GREENSBORO & ME
DANCING
THROUGH THE DECADES

A MEMOIR

Keep dancing!
Sandra Redding

GREENSBORO & ME
DANCING
THROUGH THE DECADES

A MEMOIR

SANDRA REDDING

AB
Alabaster Book Publishing
North Carolina

Copyright 2008 by Sandra Redding

All rights reserved. Printed in the United States of America. No part of this book may be reproduced in any manner whatsoever without written permission except in the case of brief quotations embodied in critical articles and reviews.

Published by Alabaster Book Publishing
P.O. Box 401
Kernersville, North Carolina 27285
www.PublisherAlabaster.biz

Book design by
David Shaffer

Cover design by
David Shaffer

First Edition

ISBN 13: 978-09815763-6-7
ISBN 10: 0-9815763-6-2

Library of Congress Control Number
2008938653

To my husband, Joe, with love and gratitude

In this book I have attempted to tell the truth about a city I love and the people who live here. I have, I believe, been successful in my task, except for one glaring omission. Though I have a sister, she asked that I not mention her in these pages. I have honored her request.

> *Dance, dance, for the figure is easy,*
> *The tune is catching and will not stop;*
> *Dance till the stars come down from the rafters,*
> *Dance, dance, dance till you drop.*
>
> > W. H. Auden

INTRODUCTION

In 2007, I served as vice-president and program chairman for Greensboro's Guilford College Chapter of AARP. When Elizabeth (Boo) Stauffer, co-chair of the Bicentennial Commission, agreed to speak to us, I was elated.

On June 13, 2007, after a fine meal served by Mahi's Restaurant, Boo stood and wowed all of us with vivid descriptions of the varied activities planned for Greensboro in 2008, the 200th birthday of the place where I've lived nearly fifty years. Even before she ended her presentation, recollections of my own history with Greensboro rushed through my mind.

After the meeting, back at home, I picked up a legal pad and began jotting down memories. As a child living in Randleman, a small Randolph County town, I perceived Greensboro to be a mecca filled with all things bright and wonderful. As I wrote, more recollections bubbled up: moving to this exceptional city with my husband Joe while in my early twenties; rearing our two sons, Joey and Mike here; growing older and wiser among friends.

In this green place, my family discovered so much that has enriched our lives, including educational and employment opportunities, entertainment, and especially the parks and hiking trails through tranquil woods. Yes, my husband and I have long treasured our dance with Greensboro. But, most of all, we remain grateful to the people here who have befriended and inspired us. This book is a tribute to them.

Dancing In Red Slippers

My earliest memory of Greensboro: a shopping trip I took with my family in 1947. I was only seven-years-old.

That chilly December afternoon, my father drove us in his battered Model-T to the big city 25 miles away. Our first stop was Sears, located on Greene Street. In comparison to the row of small shops located in Randleman, the rural Randolph County town where we lived, Sears was a huge emporium filled with gleaming appliances, elegant clothing, and, best of all, toys that whizzed and whirred.

I wanted to roam the entire store, appreciating all its treasures, but my father, tall and impatient, warned that if we kept lollygagging, we wouldn't have time to stop by Elm Street to see the Christmas decorations. My mother sighed. Taking my brother by the hand and cautioning me to "Keep up," she led us to the children's clothing department.

Then, as now, I was partial to the color red, so I pleaded for red patent leather shoes. After inspecting a pair, her luminous green eyes alert to any flaw, my mother pulled at the straps to determine how sturdy they might be. My heart pounded with excitement; I felt sure she would purchase them. Instead, she selected a plaid skirt for me and a scratchy wool sweater I detested. "You'll be glad to have it on cold mornings," she said. Oh, well, at least the color was red.

For Mick, three years younger than me, she purchased a navy sailor suit trimmed in white. I still have a picture of him wearing it. How can I help but smile when I look at the sepia-tinted photograph—such a cherubic face, his hair a mass of red curls, a smile curving his lips up just enough to reveal a dimple? In the picture I'm seated close to him. Mother always claimed that I pinched my brother as the flashbulb went off. As much as I loved him, it's hard to imagine I would be so mean. But I do admit that when our uncles gave us the change in their pockets for Christmas, I convinced Mick to trade his dimes for my nickels. "The nickels are worth more," I lied.

Before leaving Sears, we stopped by the candy counter. Though I found it difficult to select only one among all the gleaming confections displayed behind glass, I finally chose tangy lemon drops coated in sugar. Mom selected her favorite, peanut brittle, and also bought the stick of licorice Mick pointed to.

In our family, we seldom sang, except for special occasions. But, after we piled into the car, Daddy suddenly raised his deep voice, rendering *God Rest Ye Merry Gentlemen*. Soon the rest of us followed as best we could, filling the model-T with joyful though imperfect harmony. Just as we progressed to *Rudolph the Red-Nosed Reindeer*, my father swerved into a parking place in front of Belk's Department Store. Light poles down the entire street were embellished with red bows. Most pedestrians snuggled in warm winter coats. Some had on earmuffs and gloves as well. I noticed a man with a beard walking with a red striped cane. The crowd's goodwill rose up, encompassing us. Across the street, the huge Jefferson Standard Building towered so high it hurt my neck when I strained to glimpse the top. Might it fall over crushing us, I recall thinking.

My young brother giggled with delight when he saw the moving display in the Belk's Department Store window. Both of us pressed our noses against the glass, as we watched busy elves build toys and transport them in carts. If there had been a Disney World back then, at least in our minds, it wouldn't have compared with the wondrous sights we beheld as we strolled down the sidewalks of Greensboro. My mother was most impressed with Schiffman's Jewelers display. The elegant gold-rimmed china, instead of sparkling diamonds, captured her attention. As we meandered toward the front of Belk's, a scent of roasting peanuts wafted past us. How could we resist stopping at the Planter's Peanut shop? During the Christmas season Mr. Peanut, wearing a monocle and top hat, would always stand outside offering free samples. Even my father, rarely tempted by snacks, opened his large hand that evening.

In downtown Greensboro, during the late forties, there were other buildings that lured me near when our family shopped. I loved the clutter of the dime stores, F.W. Woolworth and Kress, their shelves and tables filled with whatnots, inexpensive household items, and colognes with exotic names. A fabulous tea room and stylish dresses drew women through the doors of Meyer's Department Store. My mother never allowed me to enter Montaldo's, an elegant women's clothing store. "We can't afford their prices," she whispered when we passed the storefront. "That's where *rich* ladies shop."

The centerpiece to downtown was the Carolina Theater, as classically grand as pictures I'd once seen of an Italian opera house. I never quite comprehended how the statues of two practically nude women, placed at the front on either side of the stage, managed to be selected for a North Carolina movie theater. But they definitely fit in with the maroon velvet stage curtain and the chandelier, an impressive bouquet of twinkling lights dangling from the ceiling.

On the drive home, we had to cross the railroad tracks on South Elm. The low moan of the train's whistle pricked my exuberant mood that evening. Why did we have to go back to Randleman? Why couldn't we move to Greensboro? Though the train was some distance away, my father stopped the car. While we waited, he explained how the railroad had brought opportunity and prosperity to the city.

Years later, while doing research for *Greensboro: Portrait of Progress*, a book I edited in 1998, I discovered that Governor John Motley Morehead, who made his home in Greensboro during the nineteenth century, had convinced the state legislature to locate the train's route through his hometown. According to stories I'd heard, he loved the sound of "the iron horse". To him, the rumbling locomotive signified progress. The history of Greensboro even reveals that Morehead instructed his family to bury him in a place where the train whistle could be heard.

Recently, I stood beside his grave, located in the Presbyterian Church cemetery behind Greensboro's Historical Museum. I heard the train chugging through downtown Greensboro. The soothing sound, just as Governor Morehead wished, was loud enough to be clearly identified.

I, too, love trains. As a child, whenever we stopped at railroad tracks, my imagination took wing as I wondered who might be on board and where they might be traveling. Wherever, I always concluded, it wouldn't be a place as grand as Greensboro.

What a fine evening we'd had, I thought, as we headed for home on old 220 South. My father soon began singing again. Feeling drowsy, I leaned against the door and fell asleep. Sugar plums didn't dance in my head, but, as I slept, I envisioned the red shoes that my mother had refused to buy for me. In my dream, I placed them on my feet and danced down the streets of Greensboro.

During the next week, I described my trip to friends at school. I bragged with such gusto that everyone listening must have thought I'd traveled to New York or Chicago. Still the tiniest disappointment kept creeping in. I complained to my mother: You should have bought me the shoes at Sears. Lying, I declared that every girl in my class, except me, would have red shoes on Christmas day. My practical mother answered, "There's not one thing wrong with saddle oxfords."

When she grinned, I should have guessed.

Still, I didn't find out until Christmas. That cold morning, rubbing my eyes to make sure I wasn't dreaming, I squealed when I finally looked beneath the decorated tree. There, not even wrapped in green tissue paper like the other presents, sat the red patent leather shoes. After pulling them onto my feet, I stood up and tried them out by doing the tap routine I'd recently learned in dance class. My mother laughed, a rich sound that filled every corner of the room, and, when I ended my performance with a broad smile and curtsy, my father clapped.

I've often wondered if my first impression of Greensboro would have remained so pristine if my heart's desire hadn't been realized that Christmas day?

The Missed Dance

Though I made mostly A's on my school report card during the 1950's, in some ways I remained dense as an oak tree. Several times during childhood, I failed to recognize the ugliness of prejudice. Perhaps it's because I grew up during the Eisenhower years when a strange logic called "separate but equal" was preached. We were told by politicians that blacks preferred their own schools, churches, and entertainment. They danced their own dance; we danced ours. The worst part of the ruse was the lie that what blacks had *was* equal to what we had.

By age twelve, I began to sniff out prejudice in the small town where I lived. At first, I blamed rural ignorance for racial disparity. But on trips to Greensboro, I also caught glimpses of inequality.

At Sears Department Store, there were two water fountains. The sign over the top of one stated, B*lacks*; the sign over the other, *Whites*. What did it mean? When I asked my mother, she said that I should drink from the one marked *Whites*. Why, I wondered. Was the water different? I tried the water from the

White fountain and when my mother wasn't looking, I tried the one labeled Blacks. The water tasted exactly the same. On the ride home, I told my father it was unfair. "Why do I have to choose one fountain over the other?"

"That's just the way it is, kiddo," was his answer. Though I usually accepted whatever my father said, his answer bothered me. Even then, I felt uncomfortable when another person's freedom became threatened. But it wasn't until much later that I understood how racial bias places everyone's rights in peril.

My second eye opening experience took place at the Carolina Theatre.

Occasionally, as I grew older, I'd go to a movie there, either with my parents or with a group of friends from Randleman. I always thought it unfair that blacks, lined up in an alley beside the building, were allowed to go in first. Why couldn't we go in when they did? Eventually the truth literally hit me in the head.

One hot July afternoon, I realized that once we went through the door, no blacks were visible. Not in the lobby buying popcorn. Not in the seats inside. That day, as I watched the film, something fell down across my eye. Then I thought I felt something touch my head. Reaching up, my fingers retrieved two pieces of popcorn from my thick brown hair. Another had fallen onto my lap. What was going on? Standing, I turned and looked up. Above me, there stood a group of grinning kids, their skin the soft brown of pecan shells, randomly dropping puffs of popcorn. Finally awakening from a fog of ignorance, I realized that the blacks I had seen at the side entrance must have been led to the balcony. Gradually, over time, I put the rest of the puzzle pieces together. Upstairs they obviously had a separate popcorn machine. The theater owners were more than willing to take money from black hands, yet made sure their faces wouldn't be glimpsed by white patrons.

I'm still a fan of the Carolina Theater, and remain amazed at how well it survived both literal and metaphorical fires. Still, whenever I go there to enjoy a movie or concert, I feel guilty, for I always remember the cruel treatment of blacks during earlier decades. Though the theater incident lacked the physical gravity of brutal beatings and hangings suffered by earlier blacks, it nevertheless remains an affront to human dignity that should not be forgotten nor repeated. Remembering it still makes me uncomfortable, for despite my dawning knowledge of the racial divide during my childhood, I latched onto opportunities to travel up the road to Greensboro anyway. Actually, inequality was prevalent everywhere in the South, so staying in Randleman wouldn't have provided a safe haven from injustice. Still discrimination troubled me then and continues to trouble me today.

Perhaps, because of my own heritage, one-sixteenth Cherokee, I was more prone than many to dwell on racial disparities. Greensboro, lovely in so many ways, was definitely a divided city. Downtown, the railroad tracks actually separated the white and black sections. In 1960, a sit-in, gaining national attention, took place at the whites only lunch counter of F. W. Woolworth. How much courage it must have taken for those four North Carolina A&T students—Franklin McCain, David Richmond, Ezell Blair, Jr., and Joseph McNeil— to request a cup of coffee and then refuse to leave when they weren't served. Following the example of Martin Luther King, they made tremendous strides in exposing malicious prejudice.

Remembering the event always evokes mixed emotions: I'm

proud of them and others following their example, yet ashamed that, too often, I failed to protest, march, and sit-in to foster a better community and nation for all.

During the Democratic primary election this year, the two major Democratic candidates were Barach Obama and Hillary Clinton, a black man and a white woman. How hopeful that voices of all races, nationalities, and genders now speak up, offering an olive branch for our nation. The election of John McCain as the oldest Republican candidate running for President breaks the age barrier. One day soon, I believe, all people will reach out to one another in celebration, laughing, singing, and dancing together. Now that's one party I want to attend.

Twist And Shout

During the years I attended Randleman High School, I was allowed to go to Greensboro without my parents, but because I had no car, not even a driver's license back during those dark ages of the 1950's, I took the bus. Joe Redding, a considerate young man in the grade above me, would often go along. We were a good match. I loved to talk. Nosy enough to peer through every knothole, I always had opinions. Joe, practically my opposite, listened quietly as I yakked on and on. He was the dependable one, carefully following directions and keeping us on schedule. Even then, he enjoyed taking photographs, a hobby he's held onto. When he didn't have his finger on a shutter, his head was thrown back, gazing at the sky. As a member of the Ground Observer Corp, he was responsible for watching out for any enemy aircraft flying over Randleman.

In one way we were the same: We both adored Greensboro and though our jaunts up the road would be considered mundane by today's kids, exploring the big city was, for us, as much fun as eating ice cream.

Our favorite place to dine during the late 1950's was the Mayfair Cafeteria located in downtown Greensboro. It was there I had my first taste of boiled shrimp. A shrimp cocktail still remains high on my list of preferred foods. Later, in 1960, the Mayfair became a site for controversy in Greensboro when protests by blacks took place outside the building. Later, Jesse Jackson, speaking in Montgomery, Alabama, confronted the cafeteria manager, always jovial Boyd Morris, in an anti-segregation speech. When that sad incident was reported by national media, I again recognize my own naiveté. Because I loved Greensboro so much, I often failed to see the blemishes. But the simple truth is that like most cities, Greensboro has always been and will most certainly always be an imperfect work in progress.

A special treat, when in Greensboro, was taking in a movie. There were many notable films during the tail end of the 1950s. I recall being shocked when I saw *Cat on a Hot Tin Roof* at the Carolina Theatre, and even more shocked a couple of years later when Joe and I gasped as we watched *Suddenly, Last Summer*. Elizabeth Taylor, the most talked about star of that decade, starred in both. I was spellbound by *The Rose Tattoo* starring talented Anna Magnani and *Picnic* was so delicious I saw it twice. William Holden, the male lead, was Hollywood's Mr. Dreamy back then. Because of my fondness for dancing, I had a soft spot for musicals. Despite the lackluster plot and acting, Elvis Pressley, shaking his hips in *Love me, Tender,* drew many teenagers, including me, to the theatre.

Joe, who does not enjoy shopping, willingly accompanied me as I walked through the stores and shops of downtown Greensboro. Sometimes we'd meander by Schiffman's jewelry, where I'd ogle the glittering diamonds.

Joe was more a friend than boyfriend, but within two years, our friendship flowered into love. On August 17, 1957, the summer after I graduated from high school, we married at the First Baptist Church in Randleman. Ten months later, our first son, Joseph Benjamin Redding, Jr., always called Joey by us, was born.

Those first years were not easy. When our small son was only three, the apartment we lived in caught fire. But later, in 1963, after my husband finished serving with the Army, we finally moved twenty miles up the road to our favorite city.

Before we left Randleman, I had already taken a job in Greensboro. After completing courses at the Greensboro Division of Guilford College (later the downtown Campus of Guilford Community College), I began working for International Harvester Company, located on High Point Road across from the Coliseum. That particular branch of the company sold little trucks, big trucks, and humongous trucks. In my collection of oldie photos, I have a picture of myself standing beside an enormous solid aluminum rig. In addition to the sales department, the branch also housed both parts and service departments to serve customers. At that time, approximately twenty men were employed there. I was the first female hired.

Women were definitely not treated equal in Greensboro during those years. I was expected to wear a dress or skirt and blouse to work, never pants. I was also expected to answer every telephone call. Evidently, the men didn't know how.

Once, sick with laryngitis, I could barely speak. My doctor had advised me not to talk for a couple of days. When I returned to my job that morning, I wrote a note to the office manager

Wayne Layton explaining why I couldn't answer the telephone. He said, "Answer it anyway. Even if you don't say anything, they'll tell you who they need to speak to."

Despite the inequality, I still enjoyed the eleven years I worked for International Harvester. I was paid well, had good benefits, including an excellent profit-sharing plan, which was quite a rarity then. Even more important, the men there treated me with respect. Some even offered valuable advice. After Bob McCoy, the parts manager, found that I intended to buy a new car, he explained, in a fatherly manner, how car salesmen overprice vehicles. When I decided on the car I wanted, a new blue Chevrolet sedan, he called a trustworthy salesman he knew, and then gave me pointers on how to get the best deal. Over the years Bob's wheeling and dealing how-to's served me well.

My husband also found a job in Greensboro. After he accepted a position as personnel manager for Kayser-Roth, a hosiery manufacturing plant located just off Spring Garden Street, we moved into an apartment near Lindley Park.

Though my husband and I loved being in the big city, the adjustment was not easy for our son. When we lived in Randleman, my mother, whom Joey adored, kept him while I worked. After moving, he stayed in a playschool on Market Street. Usually quiet and well-behaved, he rarely complained, still I knew the change had been difficult. Less than a year later, complicating the situation, Joey's pediatrician advised that his tonsils needed to be removed. I still remember how pale he looked when we brought him home after the surgery.

Gradually, though, he took to Greensboro. During summers, he attended an excellent day camp sponsored by the YMCA. He mastered swimming and riding horses while there. He loved being outside, so my husband and I often took him to country park to fish or ride paddle boats.

Joe and I were pleased that two couples we'd known since high school, Ione and Doug Woodlief and Nancy and Bill Poe, also lived in Greensboro. We often played Rook together or went to movies. We made new friends as well. Jack and Bernice Edwards, nearly as old as my parents, became mentors. Jack, who loved to tell jokes, worked with Joe at Kayser-Roth, and Bernice owned a clothing store on Tate Street. Joe gathered a bounty of gardening information by helping Jack plant the azaleas that filled his yard. And Bernice helped me select stylish dresses from her shop, selling them to me at a discount. Once Jack and Bernice treated us to dinner at the Carriage House, located on West Market Street, where Bert's Seafood Grille is now located.

After one meal, the cozy Carriage House instantly became my favorite Greensboro restaurant. Most of the eating establishments we frequented then no longer exist. McClure's Sky Castle, a drive-in on High Point Road, was certainly unique. The needle-shaped building, was topped by a glass enclosure. Inside a disc jockey entertained customers by playing their favorite popular songs. The most exclusive place to step out for a grand evening was Fred Koury's Plantation Supper Club. The elegant establishment looked as if it belonged in Las Vegas. Top notch singers and musicians played there and the steaks were the best in Greensboro. But a ritzy evening at the Plantation cost big bucks and fit into our budget for only the most special occasions. I can count on the fingers of one hand the times we partied there. But, oh what pleasure we derived on those rare enchanted evenings.

My husband joined the Greensboro Jaycees during the mid-

1960s. Jim Melvin, who later became the city's mayor, was also a member at that time. The group would meet for lunch at least once a month. Of the many interesting guests speaking at those lunches, Joe found "Bones" McKinney, Basketball Coach for Wake Forest, the most entertaining.

A men-only organization then, the Jaycees sponsored numerous worthwhile events, including the Greater Greensboro Open Golf Tournament. Joe remembers that he sold tickets one year and operated a concession stand another. He particularly enjoyed volunteering for the events that involved kids. One year he and Jim Peebles co-chaired the Junior Invitational Tennis Tournament. He always helped with the Soapbox Derby and had a great time taking kids from the Red Shield's Boys Club to explore a dairy farm.

Joe worked hard as a Jaycee, but the organization obviously believing "that all work and no play makes a dull boy" also provided several fun social events for members. One of their loveliest Christmas parties was held on one of the upper floors of the First Union Bank building in downtown Greensboro. All the Jaycee wives, including me, wore their fanciest dresses that evening. We feasted on food fit for kings and danced until the wee hours.

PAGA (Personnel Association of the Greensboro Area) was another organization my husband joined. Once, at a PAGA party, he introduced me to Bill Price and his beautiful wife, Joanna. They were both great dancers and we enjoyed their company that evening. Over the years we saw them often and they became treasured friends. Bill died decades ago, but we still see Joanna occasionally and she always amuses us with funny stories, just as she did the first night we met her.

During those years I had little time for organizations, but when Betty Lou Tysinger, who'd been a high school classmate, asked me to join the Lou Cecelia Chapter of the Business Women of America, I decided that being a member might help advance my career. I enjoyed the camaraderie and insights of the other members. I was also pleased that our chapter funded a scholarship to aid young women obtain college degrees.

Once a year, the chapter celebrated with a banquet, highlighted by naming one member's employer "Boss of the Year". Even then, I enjoyed writing, but being committed to family and my job with International Harvester, I rarely found a moment to sit down at my ancient Underwood typewriter and let my fingers dance across the keys. But in 1964, the day before the entry deadline, I decided to enter an essay explaining why my "boss", Max Zeirith, Manager of the Greensboro Branch of International Harvester at that time, should win the award. I still remember how good it felt to be typing something besides business letters.

The night of the banquet, when the chapter president read my essay aloud and announced that my boss had won, I was even more surprised than Mr. Zeirith. A photographer was there from the *Greensboro Daily News* to take our picture. As the flashbulb popped, a sudden glimmer of hope ignited my belief that somehow, some day, writing might actually be in my future.

The Cupcake Caper

My friend, Ione Woodlief, sewed pretty dresses for her cute daughters. And my friend, Nancy Poe, supported her sons' enthusiasm for sports by watching Tar Heel football and basketball games with them. She also attended their soccer games.

During the 1960's, I often wondered what happened to my own mothering genes. Though I desperately wanted to spend quality time with my son Joey, it rarely happened. Unlike my two friends, I did work full-time, but my husband Joe always pitched in doing more than his share of cooking and housecleaning. He even stopped by Stamey's for barbeque or Bonnie Kay's for fish every Friday evening.

Once, before he started school, I foolishly believed my son would love attending the Nutcracker Suite (Didn't everyone love dance of any kind, particularly ballet?), so I dressed him in knee pants and a white jacket and off we went. My *snakes, snails, and puppy dog tails* son wasn't impressed.

Outings with his father were more promising. They both

loved the Barnum and Bailey Circus that came to the Greensboro Coliseum each year. Once, my husband took time off from work so that Joey could see the animals and their trainers exit the railroad train and head to Spring Garden Street on their way to the coliseum.

When in elementary school, Joey went to the circus practically every year. One February he and his father had tickets for the evening performance on a cold wintry day. Though the weather forecast was dismal and light snow was already falling, they bundled up and left anyway. By the time the show ended, my husband had great difficulty finding his car, for every vehicle in the parking lot was completely covered by snow.

When Joey was eight, Joe and I decided that a dog would be a good companion for our son. When we visited the animal shelter, we fell in love with every puppy there. Knowing that any of the dogs not adopted would be euphemized made our decision even more difficult. When we finally selected a small white terrier, Joey's brown eyes sparkled and a grin as wide as a new moon brightened his face.

Unfortunately, not long after the small white dog stole our hearts, a neighborhood kid let the dog slip from his grasp. When the puppy hit the cement, we were upset. Later, when the Vet told us the dog's spine had been severed, we were inconsolable. The puppy would never be able to use his hind legs, we were told. He could never be left outside, for he couldn't protect himself. Finally, after nearly a week, I found the courage to call the Vet and let him know that we would be taking his advice: He could put the puppy to sleep.

As I watched tears fill my son's eyes that day, I realized I'd do anything to make them stop. "Joey, I think you should join Cub

Scouts," I said. "Cub Scouts spend time in the woods. They race cars in the pinewood derby, and they wear really cool uniforms covered with badges." I didn't mention that badges had to be earned.

"I can't be a Cub Scout," he protested.

"Of course, you can," I said, rubbing his bristly hair. At the time, his barber specialized in buzz cuts.

"I asked at school," he said, looking down at his shoes. "I can't be a Cub Scout, because they can't get Moms to be Den Mothers."

It was a weak moment for me. "Don't sweat it," I said. I'll be the Den Mother." Soon every Saturday morning ten eight-year-old boys clomped into my living room wearing grungy tennis shoes. One of my scouts was what's now termed *morbidly obese*. The first Saturday, he plopped down on a folding chair and the chair broke. The next Saturday I suggested he sit in an upholstered chair. He punched the arm of the chair, and it clunked to the floor. The third Saturday, I announced, "If we were real scouts, we wouldn't sit in chairs, would we? From now on, we'll sit on the floor."

Cookie Monster's chief competitor wasn't the only problem. Every boy was rowdy, so whenever possible we spent time outside. We rode paddle boats at Country Park and looked for arrowheads, which we never found. Because a large water snake hung out at Lindley Park, the guys loved to go there, hoping to spot him. As they searched, they pretended to be adventure heroes they'd read about in comic books.

Though the boys still wore stinky tennis shoes and continued to rough house, they gradually settled down once I called the session to order. And they actually enjoyed working on projects that would earn badges. To keep order, I bribed them. When they misbehaved, I scolded, "Straighten up or there'll be no refreshments."

I had been a Den Mother for almost a year when I reminded Joey that his ninth birthday would be in two weeks. "Who would you like to invite to your party?" I asked.

Mumbling through the headgear that Dr. Numa Cobb, his Orthodontist, had prescribed to help correct an overbite, he said, "Just the guys in scouts." Then looking down at his shoes, he mumbled, "Mom, would you fix real food for my birthday this year?"

"I always fix real food."

"Billy's mom made the cake for his birthday. She didn't buy one from the grocery store. She even squeezed real lemons to make lemonade." Billy was the morbidly obese kid who'd broken two of my chairs. Maybe his mom's *real food* was the problem. When I reached out to kiss Joey's head, he squirmed away from me. Escaping to the den, adjoining the kitchen, he flipped on the television to watch his favorite program, *Batman,* which broadcast every Wednesday and Thursday evening from 1966 to 1968.

A few minutes later, lured by loud noises, I walked to the den just long enough to glance at the TV screen. Batman and Robin hopped out of the Batmobile and cornered the Penguin. Batman socked the Penguin. The word POW, enclosed in a comic-strip bubble flashed onto the screen. Joey and I giggled.

An ardent procrastinator, I didn't worry about the party until the day before. After work that day, I stopped by Winn-Dixie to shop. Finally, armed with supplies, I was ready to prepare real party food to please my son. But at home, when I removed

Betty Crocker cake mix from the brown bag, Joey frowned. "Billy's mother makes his cake out of flour and eggs," he said.

"Betty Crocker is flour," I protested. "I'll add eggs."

When he spotted the cupcake papers, he asked, "What's that?"

"I thought we'd have cupcakes. That way we won't make a mess slicing the cake. And guess what? I'm icing them in your favorite color, Carolina Blue."

I detected skepticism in his smile, but he didn't protest. Instead he asked if he could watch Batman.

"Sure thing," I said, relieved to have my critic out of the kitchen. "I hope he POWS the Penguin again."

"I think he's after the Joker tonight."

I followed Betty Crocker's directions meticulously, adding eggs and water as I mixed the batter. The vanilla-scented mixture smelled homemade to me. I took out a baking sheet and placed the thin cupcake papers on it, then filled each without letting any batter slosh over the edges. After setting the oven on the specified temperature, I slipped my mini-masterpieces into the oven. As the cupcakes baked, I opened the pre-mixed icing and added just the right amount of blue food color.

Joey meandered into the kitchen. "Something smells good," he said.

His words warmed my heart. "It's your cupcakes," I told him. "In a few minutes they'll be done."

His grin was so big it almost dislodged the headgear.

Twelve minutes later I opened the oven. "What the…" I began but didn't finish the thought, thinking my son might hear. The cupcakes had melted into oblong clumps. At the time, I had no idea what I'd done wrong, but later learned that cupcake papers should always be placed into the hollows of a muffin tin.

Otherwise, the batter thins while cooking, stretching the paper holders into weird shapes.

My son hurried to the kitchen. The corners of his mouth drooped when he saw my baking disaster.

"Sorry, I messed up," I apologized.

"At first he looked as if he might cry. I wanted to cry too. Then he smiled. "Know what, Mom? They look like something on *Batman*."

"Huh?"

"Like those comic strip bubbles." We both laughed. Then, believing that somehow I could make it right, we both went to watch the rest of *Batman*. I paid close attention to each word written inside each comic bubble that evening.

After the odd-shaped cupcakes cooled, I iced them with Carolina Blue frosting.

The next day, before the party, I purchased tubes of black decorative icing and wrote a word on each cupcake. Then I made real lemonade.

For the party we had a piñata to burst and then the boys played horseshoes and Pin the Tail on the Donkey. After they were exhausted, I invited them to the kitchen for refreshments. "Wow," one of the boys said, eyeing the cupcakes: POW written on one, BAM on another, SHEZAM on a third, and SLAM on a fourth.

"Cool," Billy said.

"Yeah," Joey answered, proudly sticking out his chest. "I bet no one else's mom makes Batman cupcakes."

The Hip Hop Of Downtown

As a small child, I was first drawn to Greensboro by the glitter of downtown during Christmas. Today, Greensboro is reviving the center city, but the transition hasn't been easy. Though the popularity of downtown has hopped up and down through the decades, the center of Greensboro, at least in my opinion, has always remained a hip place to be.

The 1950s were the heyday. Then the city lured not only those in the city but also those from small nearby farm communities to drive to Greensboro to shop at elegant stores and enjoy first-class entertainment.

In August 1957, Friendly Shopping Center opened at the intersection of Wendover Avenue and Friendly Avenue. Those living nearby loved the concept. Major department stores such as Belk's and Sears located there. The center also included smaller, locally owned shops selling unique items. I still own several treasures, including a gold-trimmed ice bucket imprinted with the Dow-Jones Industrial Averages from 1958-1968, purchased there years ago at one of the center's niftiest gift shops, Potpourri.

Whether giving or attending a party, Potpourri usually had exactly what I needed. If not, I knew I'd find an even wider selection at Smith Furniture and Gift shop. Besides the large stores and the specialty shops, the center also included a number of interesting restaurants and cafes for lunch or dinner. Practically everyone, whether preferring a simple grilled cheese sandwich or a tasty Rueben, stopped occasionally by Jay's Deli. The K&W cafeteria, another popular spot, appealed to many, particularly senior citizens.

Then and now Friendly felt safe. Though many changes have taken place over the years, the congenial shopping center never lost favor with customers. Presently the center contains over 25 stores and restaurants. Many flock to the Barnes & Noble Booksellers, not only to buy books, but also to sit comfortably in the coffee shop or to attend one of the frequent book signings and readings, featuring both nationally known and local writers. The Grande movie theatre also attracts those seeking entertainment. And for the kids, there's Chucky Cheese, a restaurant featuring cartoon characters and arcade games.

From its inception, Friendly lessened the former popularity of downtown. During the late 1960's, I was torn between the two. Though I loved the convenience of shopping at Friendly, I still made frequent trips downtown. I found the architecture of the city buildings fascinating and many of the antique and art shops offered unique items at reasonable prices. I also still loved craning my neck to read the clock atop the Jefferson Standard Building. The low moan of a train shuffling its way through town still thrilled me. Because, since childhood, a piece of my heart had been invested in downtown Greensboro, I was deeply hurt as one store, and then another decided to relocate.

Still shopping had never been the main attraction of the center city. Opportunities for learning abounded in the downtown area during the latter part of the twentieth century.

My family spent many Sunday afternoons meandering through the Greensboro Historical Museum located at 130 Summit Avenue. We found the drug store display charming. After I learned about William Sidney Porter (O. Henry), Greensboro's most noted writer, by visiting the museum, I read all his books. His life fascinated me, because there had been so many contradictions. I discovered another hero, or rather heroine, in the museum, First Lady Dolley Madison, the affable wife of President James Madison. Brought up in Greensboro, Dolley Madison took her place in history with modesty and charm. One of my favorite details about her life is that she was the first woman to serve ice cream at the White House. Much as I loved the sweet confection, I had to admire her for that.

In recent years the war exhibit has been extremely popular. Poignant letters of some of those who tragically died during Wars have been preserved. The museum also celebrates surrounding areas with Seagrove pottery displays and framed arrowheads.

Another favorite learning center has always been Greensboro's Central Library, located on Church Street, and its many convenient branches scattered in neighborhoods throughout the city. Today, the library has served the community for over 100 years. Their mission, "to strive to provide free and equal access to information, foster lifelong learning, and inspire the joys of reading" is just as noble today as in the 1960's when I frequently went through those doors seeking entertainment and knowledge in books. Once, many years ago, while watching

Happy Days, a sit-com on TV, I was reminded of the value of libraries. In one episode, the Fonz, played by Harry Winkler, received his first library card. Taking it, he smiled broadly and declared, "and it's free." Following the broadcast, the number of people requesting library cards in the United States increased over 500%.

A bargain hunter, I always felt like the Fonz, bowled over that so much information and entertainment could be had without forfeiting a nickel.

We're particularly lucky here in Greensboro. Our library has continued to grow and flourish, reaching out to more and more people. In current years, the emphasis has been on *community* and efforts have been made with city-wide book discussions, Poetry Month in April, a festival of storytellers, and poetry programs to include everyone. Currently Sandy Neerman, Steve Sumerford, Suzanne Pell, Beth Sheffield and the rest of the library staff gladly welcome those who come through the library doors. Designated "the people's university", the library helps people find jobs, research genealogy, learn to use computers, and so much more. And best of all, just as the Fonz declared, "It's free!"

During the late 1960's, I particularly enjoyed taking my son Joey with me, so we could share the experience of looking at books and finally deciding which ones we'd check out to take home with us. Even then, the ambience was friendly and helpful. Puzzled, I wondered why more people didn't hang out there. Today, with the added advantage of computers to use, the library has become super active.

After one trip to the library in 1966, my son and I came closer than desired to another Greensboro institution, the Greensboro Police Department. I'd parked that day in one of the long alley of parking spaces near the bus station, located on Friendly Avenue. Anxious to get home, we hurried to the car. As I backed out, I heard a loud *crunch*. Glimpsing in the rear view mirror, I bit my lip to stop the expletive that demanded to be let out. Before I could stop my son, he rushed out and knocked on the window of the car I'd slammed into. His face was red with anger as he accused the man behind the wheel, "You hit my mother's car."

That was true enough but the other part of the truth was that I'd backed out without even checking to see if another vehicle might be behind me.

When I found out that the occupants of the other vehicle were police officers driving an unmarked car, I almost peed my pants. After a great deal of explaining to my "little hero" that his Mom was at fault, he finally caught on. Because the accident involved the police department, the street was blocked off and extensive measurements taken. Soon it looked as if most of the police department had come out to herald my little smash-up. Fortunately, I was not given a ticket, but I did have to pay for my own car repairs.

Uncomfortable as I felt trying to explain how it happened to the police officers, the real discomfort came later as I attempted to convince my husband that the accident wasn't really my fault. Because I didn't have my insurance information with me, one of the cops had already called him and ratted me out. According to my husband, the officer said, "Even after the accident, your wife backed out without looking in her rear view mirror."

Ah, well, I never claimed to be perfect.

Boogie Woogie Teddy Bear

In January 1968 my husband and I welcomed in the New Year with dancing. We had been taking lessons from Bobby Summers, a local dance instructor who operated a studio behind his house. With other friends we'd go there once a week, learning to two-step, waltz, cha-cha, tango, jitterbug. What a fun time we had.

Then in February of that year, I learned I was pregnant. Because Joey was our only child for nine years, I wondered how he would adjust to the news. One icy afternoon, soon after Joe and I told him, I walked through Lindley Park with my son. "What do you think about having a little brother or sister?"

He kicked a rock. "Well," he said, looking away, "If it's a boy, I guess it'll be okay."

"I'll do my best to come up with a little brother for you, but with babies you can never be sure," I said, touching my stomach, trying to imagine what the infant would be. I already knew I'd be happy with a boy or girl. My one wish was that the baby be healthy. Unlike now, in the 1960's, obstetricians couldn't predict a great deal ahead of time. Then, decades before the ultrasound technology offered today, having a baby became a wait and see proposition.

I didn't know how the guys I worked with at International Harvester would react to my pregnancy. Would I lose my job or would I be allowed a maternity leave? Back then, discrimination against women was common. I knew, for example, that I was still expected to wear dresses to work. Though women were gradually coming somewhat into their own, dress codes were common and casual Fridays nonexistent.

As it turned out, they urged me to work as long as I liked. When I went on maternity leave, they would hire a temp to take my place until I returned.

Though my husband and I stopped taking dance lessons, I still loved to get up and boogie when we went to Elks Lodge parties on Cornwallis Drive or to Green's Supper Club on North US 29. Later, I wondered if it might have been all my prenatal dancing that influenced my second child to be so active, once he arrived.

Shopping: One of the great joys of pregnancy. Deciding I needed to be frugal, I did a great deal more looking than buying. My husband painted the guest room a pale green, a color suitable for a boy or girl. From my mom's attic we took the baby bed that had belonged to Joey, and the high chair. Rummaging through boxes, I found baby clothes we could use. Still, even with the items that had belonged to my first son, there were still many essentials we needed.

As I toured the department stores, such as Belk's, Meyer's, and Sear's, I noticed that Winnie the Pooh seemed to be everywhere. How could I resist purchasing a cute Winnie-the-

Pooh bear? My mother gave me a blanket decorated with Winnie the Pooh for the bed. That was it, I decided. No more Winnie the Pooh. Without knowing the sex of my child, I didn't need to purchase items that wouldn't be appropriate. Still, I often thought of the adorable yellow bear wearing a red shirt and beguiling smile. Ads promoting the line frequently appeared in newspapers and magazines. He and his pals, Eeyore and Piglet, were the rage among young mothers.

By the end of my seventh month of pregnancy, my doctor suggested that I quit work to avoid toxemia, a condition that had developed with my first pregnancy. I talked to my supervisor Wayne Layton, letting him know. Later in the day, the Branch Manager Ed Maher said the guys would like to take me out to lunch on the following Friday, my last day.

We went to Stamey's, located on High Point Road, across from the Coliseum. Though the restaurant has now been expanded, it stands today on the same lot occupied in the 1960's. As we ate, a selfish thought floated through my mind: if I worked for women, they would have a baby gift for me. Of well, the barbeque was delicious. How I loved those yummy hush puppies. Later, while we waited for the peach cobblers we'd ordered, all the guys grinned. What were they up to, I wondered.

Ed shrugged his shoulders, "Well, we didn't know what to buy for a baby, so we just took up a collection." Then he handed me an envelope stuffed with ten and twenty dollar bills. I was overwhelmed.

The next day, I did some serious shopping, purchasing Winnie-the-Pooh sheets, pillow cases, lamp, night light and pictures. Thanks to the guys at International Harvester, I could buy anything and everything printed with that cute bear face.

Wisely, I held onto a few bucks for diapers.

A couple of nights later, I thought of babies as me and my gargantuan stomach waited for Mr. Sandman. Babies with blond hair or red hair or no hair all floated through my mind. Smiling babies, cooing babies, crying babies. If the baby turned out to be a boy, I thought, that would make my son happy, but if the infant were a girl, perhaps she'd take dance lessons as I'd done as a child. Maybe she'd even grow up to be a dancer. Soon, despite all those various babies, both boys and girls, dancing through my head, I fell asleep.

Before the night ended, I dreamed it was time for the baby's birth. I was already in the labor room, and Dr. Mabry, my obstetrician, was shouting at me to push. I pushed and though exhausted, I pushed again. Finally, after quite a struggle, the doctor completed the delivery. As the nurse took the baby from Dr. Mabry, she frowned. Finally, she handed the wrapped up bundle to me.

After carefully folding back a corner of the plaid blanket, I screamed.

It wasn't just a dream scream. My shrill scream woke my husband.

"What's wrong?" he asked.

"Just a bad dream."

He pulled me to him. "It must have been one awful nightmare."

"Yes," I agreed, then, after taking a deep breath, I confessed: I dreamed I gave birth to our baby."

"Really? What was it?"

"Winnie the Pooh."

On September 23, at four o'clock in the morning, real labor pains began. Getting out of bed quietly, I tip-toed downstairs, hoping I wouldn't disturb my husband. With my first-born, I suffered through labor for nearly twenty hours. Naively deciding that this pregnancy would run the same course, I figured I had plenty of time.

As it turned out, the two births shared few similarities. By the time my husband discovered that I'd gotten up, my pains were only a few minutes apart. At his insistence, I called Dr. Johnson, who was on call for Dr. Mabry. The doctor instructed me to get to the hospital immediately.

We woke our son, telling him he'd have to go with us. My husband explained, "Soon as I've helped your mother check into the hospital, I'll take you to Randleman to be with your Grandmother." While he convinced Joey to get dressed, I felt as if I were reenacting a scene from the *I Love Lucy* TV show, as I rushed about, grabbing up items I should have already packed.

When we arrived at Wesley Long Hospital, my husband explained to Joey that he'd only be a few minutes and left him in the car. Joe and I have never been certain what happened after we left, but Joey, even to this day, swears he saw a UFO.

Inside the hospital, the nurses efficiently and politely prepared me for the delivery of my second child. Wesley Long was a lovely place then. A few years ago, I was there once more for gall bladder surgery. Once again, I discovered it to be a quiet, efficiently run hospital. Though Moses Cone is considered the better hospital for major surgery, Wesley Long, because it's smaller, gets thumbs up from me when it comes to tender loving care.

After wheeling me into the delivery room, a doctor gave me

a shot of "feel good." Nothing, not even giving birth to a stuffed animal, could have upset me. Totally relaxed by the anesthetic, I told Dr. Johnson about my Winnie-the-Pooh dream.

He chuckled. "Well, giving birth to a stuffed bear might actually be easier on the mother," he answered.

That's all I remember until at least an hour later. By that time I lay on a stretcher, my husband standing beside me. "Well?" I asked.

He grinned broadly. "We have another healthy boy."

How much does he weigh?" I asked. Joey had weighted only 5 lbs, 7 ounces at birth. I'd been determined to have at least a six pounder this time.

My husband took my hand. "5 pounds, 15 ounces."

"Oh, shoot."

After the nurses settled me into a room, they brought my baby. Though small, he appeared to be absolutely perfect. Dark hair covered his head. How wonderful it felt to have an infant in my arms again. All felt right with the world, but by the next afternoon, my emotions took a nose dive.

Unlike now, during the dark ages, hospitals didn't allow children under the age of twelve to go inside for visits. I was absolutely furious when I learned I wouldn't be seeing Joey. Furthermore, after a delivery, new mothers were required to stay in the hospital at least four days. As I stood at the window, my oldest son standing three stories below, my heart almost broke. He waved; I waved. Smiling he mouthed, "I love you, Mom." Feeling a surge of tears, I turned away. I suppose it must have been postpartum depression, a condition that was never mentioned then. I do know that for the next two days, I was in a dark place, feeling as if I'd deserted my sweet-natured

Joey.

My thoughtful husband brought me roses, yet despite the fragile beauty and sweet scent of his gift, I still felt a great sense of loss. The two of us had already decided if we had a boy, we'd name him Michael. My brother, who I always loved so much, was named Michael. I never regretted naming my son after him, for he never had children of his own. My husband selected our son's second name: Kent. I liked the sound of it and to my own brain, *Kent* connoted strength and integrity.

Then as now, I avidly read the hometown newspaper. As I made my way through the pages of the *Greensboro Daily News*, one feature designated "House of the Week" caught my eye. The home displayed was an impressive two-story brick with a kitchen, formal dining room, living room, three bedrooms, two and one-half baths, and the piece de resistance, a large den with an oval brick fireplace.

For months Joe and I had planned to start looking for a house to buy. Since moving to Greensboro, we had moved from an apartment at 1100-A Willowbrook Drive to an attractive small rental house at 4108 Ashland Drive. Soon as my husband came to the hospital that evening, I showed him the picture and article featuring my "dream home."

He, too, was impressed.

The next morning, when he arrived at the hospital to take me and our new son home, he told me he had contacted the builder of the house pictured in the newspaper.

"Well," I asked, "when can we go see it?"

"It's already been sold."

My heart plummeted until I noticed the grin brightening his face. "They're getting ready to build another one like it, but in another neighborhood."

"What a great day," I thought as on the drive home, I held my tiny new baby tightly. Even though he was *a snakes, snails, and puppy-dog tail* boy, he smelled of everything nice.

Once at home I placed our new son in a wicker bassinet, the small mattress covered with a Winnie-the-Pooh sheet. Two hours later, Joey, arrived home from school. After giving him a big hug, I said, "Go take a look at your baby brother. He's in the bassinet."

Walking cautiously across the room, he took a peek and jumped back. Because he'd never seen an infant so small, he thought that something must surely be wrong with Michael. We explained how all babies were small at first and that his new brother was fine. Still, at first, Joey was cautious about holding Mike and playing with him. Soon, though, he found out how tough infants can be and the two have remained great pals ever since.

Doing The Two Step

If, as one song says, "One is the loneliest number", loneliness wasn't a possibility for my family during the next few years. My husband and I now had two sons instead of one. And I had two jobs: caring for my family and continuing to work for International Harvester. Another duality during those years was remembering that "all work and no play makes Joe and Sandra a dull couple", so though both my husband and I stayed busy during the work week, we did reserve time for fun with our boys on weekends.

Joe and I also occasionally kicked up our heels with friends, usually by attending a dance at the Elks Lodge on Cornwallis Drive. The food was always scrumptious. We particularly enjoyed the luau held there each summer. Centering the table would be a cooked pig, an apple stuck in its fat mouth. Many of the women dressed in muumuus and leis and the men wore brightly colored Hawaiian shirts. Later, after dinner, a band played. We particularly enjoyed the evenings when Burt Massengale's group entertained. Over the years Burt became a

Greensboro institution. The broad grin he wore remained, as if glued to his face, even when he was asked for the tenth time to play, *Joy to the World,* better known as that bullfrog song by the crowd we hung out with. We usually sat at a long table with Nancy and Bill Poe, Betty and Bob Whitley, Betty and Henry Peraldo, and Joanna and Bill Price. We also enjoyed partying with Jeanette and Gordon Windham, Fran and Tim Lambeth, and Jimmy and Faye Harrell. Most of us were full of foolishness and ginger.

Soon as construction was completed on our new house at 3312 Winchester Drive, we moved in. I shopped for just the right furniture and accessories, unwilling to pay more than bargain prices. My husband labored diligently, landscaping the yard. He planted scarlet azaleas that bloomed gloriously every spring. We both loved the sight of bright golden spears of forsythia extending skyward, so he planted several bushes along the back of our property. On the right side of the house, red leaf plums divided our property from our neighbor's. The most spectacular trees in the yard were the dogwoods my husband's employer, Alan Johnson, had allowed him to remove from his land. Delicate as bridal lace, the white blossoms softened the landscape.

We liked our neighbors, and our sons had many playmates while we lived there. One neighbor, Phyllis Snider, owned the ceramic shop where I went for R&R every Tuesday evening. During that time I made several items for gifts and for my own home. For a while, my friend Nancy Poe went with me and we had great fun talking about our kids as we created miniature works of art. Once, getting overly ambitious, I made huge chess pieces, which I painted blue and green. It would be a surprise for my husband. Once I finished the Kings, Queens, Bishops, Knights, and Pawns, I painted tiles I planned to glue to a table for the chess board. When I finished, I felt sure that I had just the right gift for Joe. He didn't tell me then, but later, when I asked why he seldom used the chess table, he explained that the way the chessmen were painted, each partially green and blue, it was difficult to identify his own men. He was happier playing with an inexpensive plastic set.

In previous years and the ones following that mistake, I frequently erred in a similar way. My husband saw no reason to *gild the lily*. His "Quaker" mentality was to purchase or make what worked without going to a great deal of expense. He still purchases his watches from drugstores, claiming to prefer them to all others. I've actually come to admire that trait, even adopted it to a degree.

Still, during those early years, our differences sometimes collided. After moving into our new home, I often plowed through magazines looking for unusual accessories that fit my vision. Once I purchased a white wicker birdcage, hanging it on a chain over the commode in our downstairs bathroom. I filled it with silk ivy. Recently, I came across a photo my husband made of my decoration. "Oh my, how tacky," I thought.

Soon after I installed the birdhouse, we threw a party for friends. Before they arrived, Joe mixed up a punch containing Southern Comfort and I put out potato chips and French Onion dip, a platter of veggies and a platter of fruit and cheese. I learned two lessons that evening: Southern Comfort in punch means a headache the next morning, and when you have company, a thorough house cleaning is more important than gilding the lily. Actually the house was quite clean. My husband had made sure of that, but because I'd wasted my time on unnecessary details, such as arranging flowers I'd picked from the yard and placing soap balls in ceramic dishes, I didn't leave enough time to fold and put away the clothes I'd taken out of the dryer. When the doorbell rang that evening, I simply gathered up the laundry I'd placed on the sofa, intending to take care of it at the last minute, and tossed it into the tub in the downstairs bathroom. As I closed the shower curtain, I convinced myself that no one would notice.

When I answered the door, our friend Bill Price, an expert at ferreting out a person's flaws, stood there with his lovely wife Joanna. After the other guests arrived, Bill used our bathroom. All of us heard his loud laughter. Was he making fun of that danged wicker birdhouse I'd taken so much time making, I wondered?

Exasperated, I confronted Bill later. "Just because you don't appreciate art is no reason to make fun of my birdcage."

All the guests gave me that look, the one indicating, "Honey, I think you might have had too much of your own punch."

Finally, a mischievous gleam lighting his blue eyes, Bill said, "Let's all go the bathroom together." Once inside, he opened the shower curtain revealing my laundry to one and all.

That was so typical of him. Both he and his wife loved to laugh. Once, he asked for my broom. When I asked why, he pointed to the ceiling, "You missed a few cobwebs." Another time, when I served lasagna to him and Joanna, he dramatically kept hacking away at the pasta. Finally, I asked, "Well, what is it this time, Bill?" Turns out I'd carelessly included a piece of paper used to separate the slices of mozzarella cheese in my unfortunate recipe.

Bill Price died over two decades ago, but Joanna still lives in Greensboro. Whenever we bump into one another at a social event or while shopping, I grin, anxious to hear the humorous story I'm sure she'll relate to me. As we chat about *old times*, I often think of Bill, always amusing us with his wry observations.

The most special times, during the years we lived on Winchester Drive, were at Christmas. We loved taking the kids to downtown Greensboro for the parade. We'd also go every year to Friendly Shopping Center. I kept a special place in my heart for the large plaster Santa Claus the shopping center always placed at the corner of Friendly Avenue during December. When my kids were small we'd always wave to him. For many years, the customer service building of Friendly Center displayed trees, each one decorated by a different Garden Club in Greensboro. Though the trees are now displayed each Christmas season in a building beside the Environmental Center, going to see the exhibit still ignites the Christmas spirit for me.

During the holidays, Santa Claus still sits on his throne in the Friendly Service Center, eagerly prompting nervous kids to tell him what they'd like him to bring. Their reactions vary. When we took our granddaughter Amber, at age three, she remained tentative. Though she refused to sit on his lap, she did tell him what she expected him to show up with on Christmas morning. Now, at age six, she's no longer intimidated by the bearded big guy.

Another treat for customers that Friendly Shopping Center has added in recent years is the carolers, dressed in Victorian costumes, singing seasonal songs. And, as always, Salvation Army volunteers still stand in the cold outside stores, ringing a bell, reminding that "giving is what Christmas is all about." Who, besides an absolute Scrooge, could resist dropping at least a coin or two into each kettle?

A yearly tradition our family established several years ago is to reserve one night of the holiday season to drive around the city, searching for spectacular Christmas decorations. For years, a small house on Chapman Street kept every nook and cranny of their yard and roof bright with lights and ornaments. Now, with the advent of those huge colorful balls, made of wire and filled with strings of lights, some of Greensboro's streets become magical wonderlands during the holiday season. Joe and I also love walking the campus of the University of North Carolina in Greensboro or following the path through the Arboretum on nights when luminaries are lit.

Indeed, Greensboro is a spectacular place to be in December, though I can't recall a single Christmas, during my lifetime, when it snowed on Christmas day.

While we lived on Winchester Drive, the Christmas tree in our house had the same theme each year. Always we'd have white lights and lots of silver icicles dripping from the branches. The ornaments included those made by our children and my husband. During one holiday season, after I returned home from shopping for presents, I found Joe, who'd been watching the kids, doubled over by pain. I rushed him to the hospital, after calling Nancy and Bill Poe to come look after Joey and Mike. A kidney stone turned out to be the culprit. Unable to work for a few days, Joe occupied his mind by painting wooden tree ornaments. Every year, I still hang the ones he painted on our tree. And every year, I also hang up the red felt ornaments my husband and youngest son made in Indian Guides: Joe's says Big Moon; Mike's says Little Moon. At that time, I also collected white dove ornaments and on the very top, instead of a traditional angel, we hung a large silver Peace symbol, for even during those years when our country wasn't at war, our family prayer has always been for world peace.

Christmas morning, my husband and I would quietly descend the stairs. After building a roaring fire in the den fireplace, we'd place the gifts for our boys under the tree and light the angel chimes. Finally we'd sit down with mugs of French Roast coffee and eat the sugar cookies Mike left for Santa. These peaceful moments never lasted long, for soon the children woke, bounding down the stairs, anxious to find what Santa brought.

As much as I looked forward to Christmas mornings, I loved Christmas evenings ever more. In the afternoon we'd have dinner with my family in Randleman and afterwards go by to visit Mom and Pop Redding. Then, happy but tired, we'd drive back to Greensboro. Michael would be in the front seat close to me and Joey would be in the back seat. Always without fail, some time during that ride home, my eldest son would lean forward, touching our shoulders and say, "This is the best Christmas I've ever had."

Those years were busy, yet magical. Few experiences can compare with watching children grow and change. As they learn something new, it's as if you, too, are learning again, in a slightly different way. When Michael walked at nine months I was amazed. Watching him, I recognized the complexity of placing one foot in front of the other without losing balance. Even today, when I observe my youngest granddaughter Emily walking, I'm reminded, once again, of the value that remaining mobile adds to life. Too often, in this country, we speak of exercise as a chore. For most people, the joy of walking and other physical activities isn't fully appreciated until mobility is lost. In my opinion Greensboro should issue an ordinance requiring all able-bodied citizens to walk at least thirty minutes each day. Hey, maybe they should also require everyone, especially reluctant husbands, to dance as well.

The Grapevine

In dance, the grapevine is a classic traveling step

In 1971, my husband accepted a new position. He would be working for Cecil Sherman who managed Rolane, a group of outlets stores that sold Kayser-Roth products as well as other brands of merchandise. The outlet business boom had taken hold in the Northeast, so when Joe joined up with Cecil, there were many opportunities for advancement. He decided it was a job he couldn't refuse.

From the first time I met him, I admired Cecil Sherman. A gregarious man, he was tall and had a laugh that conveyed high spirits. Though he required a great deal of those working for him, he enjoyed entertaining his employees in his home, located in Burlington, or taking them out to dinner. Cecil took my husband and me to some of the finest restaurants in North Carolina. We particularly loved going with him to Jacque's in Greensboro. The cozy restaurant featured innovative cuisine and lively entertainment, including music and a dance floor for those wishing to trip the light fantastic.

Though I thought my husband made a wise career decision,

the evening he explained that we would need to move to Alamance County, where Rolane's headquarters were located, stunned me.

Immediately everything I would miss about Greensboro came to mind. I loved getting up early on Saturday mornings to go to the Farmer's Market on Yanceyville Street. For years farmers had gathered there with fresh vegetables and beautiful flowers. I would also miss going to movies with friends and attending the dances at the Elks Lodge and going to Greene's Supper Club for fried oysters. Most of all we'd miss the many close friends we had in Greensboro. What about Joey, I wondered. Like me he would have to adjust, making new friends.

Still, I knew that moving would be the right decision.

That night my husband and I made another bold choice. We decided that I should quit working after the move and stay home with our youngest child Michael. Until he was almost three, a wonderful older couple, Mr. and Mrs. Wright, had kept him. But for more than a year, since we'd placed him in a play school while we worked, he'd had a series of ear infections. My hope was that keeping him from close contact with sick children would break the cycle. Change, I tried convincing myself, would be good for all of us. Still my heart ached when I thought of leaving Greensboro.

The Alamance County town that we chose for our home was Elon College (now called Elon). A charming small town blessed with a fine college within its city limits, we'd be only thirty minutes from Greensboro, a good thing, for I intended to drive back to my favorite city often.

I suppose I sound like a Goody Two-Shoes when I call Greensboro my favorite city. Admittedly, there are flaws here just as everywhere else. Racial prejudice existed all my life, even in Greensboro. And in Greensboro, the rich often seem to get richer and the poor poorer just as in other places. But, I'm still convinced, that if hearts could be read, it would be discovered that Greensboro has a phenomenally high percentage rate of good-hearted citizens. This belief was substantiated two days before our move to Elon.

I'd stopped by First Union Bank, withdrawing $250.00, that warm August day. I'd found that my spending habits were more controlled if I put aside a specified amount for shopping. To me, if checks or credit cards were used, it seemed as if real money had not been spent. It's a silly little game I played back then. But when I actually watched dollar bills fly from my hand and into the cash register, I couldn't be fooled. Then I knew for certain the money was gone.

My first stop was at the Rolane store in Greensboro. While there I purchased socks for my sons and a pair of pedal-pushers for myself. Large lime green pillows caught my eye. I purchased two to brighten a sofa I'd recently had reupholstered in a hound's-tooth print. Before leaving I dropped by my husband's office to chat with him. I had two large bags filled with items when I reached the parking lot. Because I'd only spent $55, I still had nearly $200 in my purse. Getting in my Chevrolet, I headed home. Once there, I discovered that my purse, containing my driver's license, credit cards and money was missing. I felt absolutely heart sick. Where could I have left it? Then I remembered: I'd put my purse down on the asphalt parking lot, so that I could place my cumbersome packages in the car. I couldn't remember picking it back up. Getting in the car, I rushed back to the store. No purse, not anywhere.

I dreaded telling my husband when he came home. Someone might already be using my credit cards, I thought. Someone might be spending my hard-earned money. Before I unlocked the front door of my house, I heard the phone ring.

When I answered, an unfamiliar voice asked my name. I hesitated, but then said, "I'm Sandra Redding."

"And where do you live?" The voice demanded.

"Why do you want to know?" I asked.

"I found something that might belong to you."

My heart lifted. Maybe I would get my purse back. After giving my address, the woman explained. "When I left Rolane, I saw a pocketbook in the parking lot. Afraid that someone dishonest might pick it up, I brought it home with me." She gave me her address. I thanked her profusely and asked when it would be convenient to pick it up.

"Anytime will be fine," she answered. "My children just got home from school, so I'm not planning to go anywhere."

I rushed through traffic. The address I'd been given was located in one of the poorer sections of town. Soon as I knocked, a woman wearing a faded dress and bedroom slippers opened the door. "I'm sorry to cause you so much trouble," I apologized

Tall and thin with compassionate brown eyes, she told me that she always had time to help others.

"I'm lucky to be the recipient."

I heard children's voices. Inviting me inside, she introduced me to each of them. "Half a dozen," she joked. Their ages ranged from four to twelve.

I looked around. The small living room was neat except for a pile of clothes on the worn sofa. "I've been catching up with the ironing," she explained. I noticed how worn the clothes were.

She reached behind the sofa. Retrieving my straw purse, she handed it to me. Though enormously grateful, I'm ashamed to admit that another emotion, dark and ugly, squirmed inside my head. Would all my money be there? With all those kids needing supplies and clothes for school, how could the woman not be tempted? Slyly, I opened my purse and counted: $195.00.

"I hope it's all there," she woman said, "I don't know how long your purse had been left in the parking lot."

"All accounted for," I said. Then I took two twenty dollar bills and handed them to her.

"No," she said. "I wasn't expecting anything."

"I planned to place an ad," I told her, "I would have offered a reward. I worried about the loss of the money, but I worried even more about someone using my credit cards and checks."

Smiling, she thanked me. Then one of her children, a small child with enormous dark eyes, joined in, chanting, "Thank you. Thank you."

Wonderful words, I thought. Then *thanking her*, I left.

Every day I read of burglaries and rapes and murders in Greensboro. And every day, I'm astounded. Where does it happen? I wonder. During the years I've lived here, I've only had two items taken from me. One was a jumbo bag of potato chips and the other a satchel containing books and papers which I'd carelessly left in an unlocked car.

Have I just been exceptionally lucky? I doubt it. Given the population of Greensboro and the current lack of responsibility that seems to have settled over our society, crimes are bound to happen. Still, in my opinion, Greensboro remains a safe place to live. And if something bad does happen, neighbors and friends can be counted on to pitch in and help.

The morning the movers arrived, I, once again, counted up all that I'd miss. Friends were at the top of the list. Then there were the parks, favorite places to shop and be entertained. Our house? Yes, I'd miss that too, I thought, as my husband and two sons walked across the yard with me one last time. It was the first one we'd owned, and during the six years we lived there, we'd been happy and content.

But it would be okay, I'd almost convinced myself, until I came to the spruce tree in the side yard. The previous December, it had been the Christmas tree inside our house. After the holidays, my husband planted it in the yard. When I touched one of the branches, I saw a Christmas decoration I'd failed to remove. A single silver icicle, bravely blowing in the breeze, still clung to one of the needles. When I reached out touching it, I was no longer able to stop the tears that suddenly welled up in my eyes.

Doing The Locomotion
In this line dance, participants step forward, and then back again

During the years we lived in Elon, I never quite let go of Greensboro. Because we were only thirty miles away, I found numerous excuses to get on Highway 70 and whiz back to the place I considered home base.

Still there would be benefits. Since I was no longer working, I would have more time to spend with my sons. I also had time to finally contemplate on the person I wanted to be. At first I was gung ho with creating a happy home life for our family. I prepared interesting meals. I wanted to decorate the home we bought. Though not quite as large as the house we'd owned in Greensboro, it was comfy and practical. At the top of my agenda was mirroring the living room wall so that the room would appear bigger. Against the smoky mirrored wall, my husband and I placed an off-white velvet sofa fronted by a glass-topped table. On either side were two red velvet chairs. Then, I thought it was so chic. Thinking of it now, I realize that it was overdone and certainly not a practical room for the children.

While living in Elon, I became President of the recently

formed neighborhood garden club. I also joined a bridge club, an activity that became addictive. At first, I played with three neighborhood women each Wednesday morning. Rotating as hostess, we would serve something simple, such as coffee and Danish. Soon we extended the hours of our weekly sessions, playing until lunch, which would be served by the hostess for that day. Then after a month or so, our bridge game mushroomed, and we would still be playing when our kids arrived home from school. Finally, completely succumbing to the cards in the deck, we played until our husbands, returning from work, closed our gambling den down. We also indulged in other neighborhood get-togethers, such as a Happy Hour on Friday afternoons.

During those years, Diane Gash, who lived next door, became my best bridge buddy. I also enjoyed conversations with Martha Smith who lived across the street. She taught English at Elon College, and I loved hearing her descriptions of the European trips she'd taken. She also recommended books that I might enjoy reading.

Joey quickly adjusted to the school, and Michael stopped having ear infections. Being with him all day was great fun, but exhausting. He had more energy than any child I've ever been close to, except, perhaps, for his daughter Amber. Always friendly and lively, he feared nothing. Every chance he had, he would be on his big wheel making a mad dash down the driveway. Though warned not to go into the road, he sometimes did. Fearing for his safety, I'd scold him when he failed to listen.

A year later, he went through a period of developing his pitching arm with unfortunate results. One afternoon, he and his equally exuberant friend, Johnny Fletcher, tossed small stones breaking several windows of the building at the end of street, an old church where Woodmen of he World held meetings.

As I prepared dinner that evening, the doorbell rang. When I answered, a police officer stood in front of me. He asked, "Does Michael Redding live here?" At the time, Mike was only five years old.

What is it?" I asked.

Then he explained the broken windows. An elderly woman had witnessed the crime. Michael was grounded and my husband spent many hours replacing the broken window panes. Though I found it painful to watch Mike staring sadly out the window of his room, I insisted that, for punishment, he remain inside the house for a week. Soon after we allowed him to play outside again, he broke another window while tossing a ball. One of the neighbors telephoned me. "Well," she said, "Michael's done it again."

It was too much. I lay down on the sofa, a vision in my head of my son in a reformatory school, attempting to break windows there.

The move affected my boys in many ways, most positive, I believe. Joe grew to love living in Alamance County. He still lives there today. Living in a different place changed me as well. Finally, at the age of 33, I could pause long enough to decide what direction I'd like my life to take. The inkling of possibility first occurred to me when I enrolled in a Mature Woman seminar given at Alamance Technical College in Burlington. The psychologist leading the course gave us a battery of tests and we wrote essays defining what meant most to us. In a conference, near the conclusion of the seminar, the instructor pointed out that I should be a librarian or a teacher or writer.

The next semester I enrolled in a Creative Writing course at the community college. After completing the first class, I was hooked. We wrote short stories, poems and essays. When I read my work to the class, the other students encouraged me. One of my classmates, Leon Hinton, mentioned that Burlington had an active writing club. He convinced several of us taking the course to join.

Leon, now in his eighties, has changed little over the years. I still enjoy seeing him when I attend the annual North Carolina Writer's Conference held each July. At eighty-one, he's still witty, wise, and has most of his hair. What I admire most about Leon is that he still takes the time to encourage other writers. I also like that his own stories, essays, and poems reveal so much of his own personality. Once, during a reading, to better illustrate an essay he'd written about sleep disorders, he played a recording of himself snoring loudly (a quite dreadful sound). Everyone in the room laughed heartily. Even Leon couldn't keep a straight face.

All my life I'd loved reading and in high school, I wrote articles for the school newspaper, but growing up in the small town of Randleman, I'd never even met a writer. The writers I loved most, Thomas Wolfe and Walt Whitman, had left the earth many moons before. I suppose I assumed that writers lived on Mount Olympus. But in the Burlington Writers Club, I finally met writers who had won prizes for their efforts. A few had even been published.

The same year that my interest in writing peaked, I took a temporary job as a file clerk with the Employment Security Commission of Alamance County. A young man who wrote poetry was also hired there a month or so later. Because he knew I loved to read, he brought his poems for me to critique. One day, a story popped into my head that I felt compelled to write. I wrote all night, unwilling to quit and go to bed. What if I lost the thread of the story, I feared. What if the muse disappeared and I couldn't complete what I had started? The next morning, sleepy but pleased, I took my story to work and requested that the "Poet" read it and let me know what he thought. The next day, when he told me he liked it, I was ecstatic. That day he also gave me advice for which I shall be forever grateful. "If you are serious about writing, you need to get an education."

Taking his advice literally changed my life. Moving to Alamance County had given me some time to think about what I wanted to do with the rest of my life and his words became my map. "Yes," I remember thinking, "I did want to write." I knew, that given my situation, I would have been wiser to decide to be a nurse or a teacher, but wisdom couldn't change the way I felt. In my heart, I knew I was a writer. How could I continue to reject that calling?

Six years after we moved to Alamance County, my husband accepted the position of Operations Manager for the group of Belk's Stores then in Greensboro. This included the downtown store, the Friendly Shopping Center Store, and the ones at Four Season's and Carolina Circle Malls. Though I'd always dreamed of moving back to Greensboro, my emotions were mixed. There were so many people I'd miss in Alamance County: my neighbors, friends in the Burlington Writers Club, and friends and instructors at Alamance Community College where I'd taken several courses.

By the time we left, my best friend Dianne Gash and her family had already moved to Orlando, Florida, so that made it a bit easier. After she moved away, my husband, as a Valentine's Day gift, had bought plane tickets so Michael and I could fly down to see her and her youngest son Stuart, who had been Michael's best buddy. During that week, we had a great visit, catching up as we took the kids to Disney World, Seaworld, and Busch Gardens. Always generous, she wanted to make sure we enjoyed a large slice of Florida.

Uncertain where we wanted to live in Greensboro, we initially moved into a condominium located in Bramblegate. My interest had flip-flopped by that time. No longer obsessed with decorating a house or cooking meals, I started a new chapter entirely. I wanted an education and I wanted to be a writer. The stumbling blocks: I was almost thirty-six years old and my eldest son would soon be going to college.

At first, I worked at several temporary positions. We met and became friends with our neighbors, and my youngest son joined a scout troupe. We were proud of him for earning badges and for participating in a 50-mile hike. We were even more impressed that in his every day behavior he lived up to the scout code.

Once, after picking my son up from a scout meeting on a snowy afternoon, the car slid on ice, rear-ending the vehicle in front of us. I watched, petrified, as the driver slumped down in the seat. Mike immediately shot out of our car and rushed through the snow to the damaged vehicle. Knocking at the window, he kept repeating, "Are you all right?" Fortunately the woman was not seriously injured, but if she had been, I'm sure my son would have administered CPR, if necessary.

Joey, my eldest, never quite got over the move back to

Greensboro. He reluctantly enrolled at the University of North Carolina in Greensboro, but still made frequent trips to Alamance County. Love had bitten him; he had a girl friend. Before the school year ended, he dropped out. I recall one heated conversation we had. I became very angry, outlining all the reasons that getting an education was essential. Finally, he said back to me: "If it's that important, why don't you go?"

And so I did.

I was terrified the day I first went to the university to talk to an advisor. What if they turned me down? Though I had taken courses at both the Greensboro Division of Guilford College and at Alamance Community College, I felt sure that the university would be different. When I went to high school, SAT's weren't given. Would I have to take an SAT? I wondered. If so, would I score high enough to be accepted?

During the interview, I became less apprehensive as Barbara, a woman who appeared very competent, explained the contingency program recently adopted by the university. I could attend my first year and if my grades remained acceptable, I would be allowed to continue. An orientation was recommended and, of course, I attended. Like many adult students returning to the classroom years after graduating from high school, I became an over achiever, determined to do whatever necessary to succeed.

I majored in English, never fearing the literature courses, but courses in math made me shiver in my espadrilles. Fortunately, tip-toeing around math courses was a possibility. I could, for instance, take a psychology course that concentrated on statistics to receive math credit.

With gratitude, I accepted that option. I must have thought

there was a trick to it, for I worried endlessly about passing the course. I still recall studying long hours for the first test. We would have only three chances to prove what we knew during that semester, so passing the first examination was crucial.

Sitting at my desk the morning of the test, I felt that I might throw up. When I picked up my pencil, my hand shook. How would I manage to write? Then I had an idea. I grasped my right wrist tightly with my left hand, to steady it, as I scribbled out answers. Fortunately most of the questions were multiple choice. Still my short answer responses looked quite peculiar, as if someone at least ninety must have written them. But penmanship didn't matter. I made an A on my psychology course and on every other subject I attempted my first semester.

English courses continued to nurture me. I felt like a bird being fed tidbits of knowledge. I was hungry to know everything about the writers I most admired. I fell absolutely in love with Chaucer. I liked that his stories were wise, witty, and scandalous. To pass the course we were required to write a paper on Chaucer or one of his stories. I suppose it must be a character flaw, but I always have difficulty with being told what to do. Thinking I had a better idea than the required paper, I asked my instructor if I could write a sonnet relating to the course material instead.

He laughed, apparently amused by such a preposterous idea. "I'll give you the grade you deserve," he let me know. "Sonnets are difficult. It would be easier to write a paper." But, finally, reluctantly, he relented, allowing me to have my way. I wrote a sonnet entitled "The Wife of Bath."

He found it entertaining. In a conference, he explained that the sonnet didn't scan in a couple of places, and then he had to explain to me what he meant. I fixed it and made an A. Later I submitted my sonnet to the Sidney Lanier Division of the North Carolina Poetry Society's contest. It won first place and I was presented a huge trophy and publication. Still I'd learned that *yes*, my professor was correct, sonnets are difficult to write. I never attempted one again.

The music of possible success transported me though the years I worked for my undergraduate degree. I never allowed myself to believe that I couldn't do it, and I remained insistent on doing it my way.

A busy schedule didn't leave much time for becoming friends with my fellow classmates. However, I did become close to a few. One of them, Bonnie Miller, who went on to complete work on her graduate degree at the University of North Carolina in Chapel Hill, is now a social worker in Greensboro. Though we lost touch for several years, we now meet for lunch occasionally.

I love chatting with Bonnie. Always enthusiastic and open to new ideas, I recall that when we were both taking classes at UNC-G, she once drove me in her Porsche to Winston-Salem, where she treated me to lunch. Now, when we *do* lunch, we enjoy Panera on Battleground Avenue or Vito's, located in Golden Gate Shopping Center. Both restaurants serve tasty soups and salads. Because the ambience is casual at these two eateries, they provide perfect places to enjoy good food while Bonnie and I catch up with one another's lives.

While I attended school, I worked at various temporary jobs during school breaks and in the summer. One summer I worked at Western Electric, then located on Highway 40 between Greensboro and Alamance Country. My employers were company attorneys, and I enjoyed chatting with them about law and about books. One of the attorneys introduced me to the writing of Yukio Mishama. Once I started reading Mishama's exquisitely crafted fiction, he became one of my favorite writers.

On Saint Patrick's Day, the attorneys took everyone in the department out to a nearby restaurant. It was a special experience because three of the attorneys were Irish. After we finished lunch, the Irishmen sang songs of their homeland. I was particularly touched with their heart-felt rendition of *Danny Boy*. One of them actually had tears in his eyes.

After I completed my second year at the University and began the fall semester of my third year, my husband left Belk's and resumed working once more for Rolane Factory Outlets. Initially he managed the Greensboro store, but was soon offered a promotion, District Manager of stores in Tennessee, Alabama, Georgia, and South Carolina. The logical place for us to live would be in the Atlanta area of Georgia. My heart sank. What would I do about getting my degree? I'd worked so hard. There was no way I could explain to him or to anyone else how much it meant to me.

We were to fly to Atlanta to look at houses. I was petrified at the idea of leaving Greensboro, not only for myself, but also for Michael, our son, who was in the middle of the school year. Still how I could I disappoint my husband? The promotion meant so much to him. I drove around Greensboro the day before flying to Atlanta. I went by many of my favorite haunts. I parked at Yum-Yums, an ice-cream parlor on Spring Garden. I bought a cone of Chocolate. Then I walked the campus of the University, barely able to hold back the tears. I passed "Charlie", the statue of the University's founder, Charles Duncan McIver. Later I meandered into the library, my very favorite place, going up to one floor, then another. I'd spent many hours studying there. That had been a joyful focused time. With my nose in a book, I forgot all else. I loved how the stacks smelled of history and romance. Always a warm place, a cocoon where solitude could be found and my own thoughts could rule. How could I give it up without getting my degree?

The flight to Atlanta was awkward. Feeling distant and aloof, I was unable to share my husband's enthusiasm. Finally, that evening, as Joe and I had dinner at a fine restaurant, the way out of my dilemma became as clear-cut as a laser beam: I didn't have to move. I could stay in Greensboro until the end of the school year. This decision was not an easy one. My husband would be disappointed. He might even refuse to understand. Nevertheless, that's what I felt I had to do, and so, with my heart in my throat, I told him.

My son and I lived on in Greensboro until Mike finished his fifth grade in school and until I finished my junior year at the University. Once we moved, I would be able to finish work for my B.A. by taking courses at Kennesaw College in Marietta, Georgia and by completing a correspondence course in Shakespeare's plays offered by the University of North Carolina at Chapel Hill. That would leave only three required courses, but I could return to Greensboro for a short summer semester to take those. It was a patchwork way to earn my B.A., but the only way.

A final, seemingly indomitable hurdle was that during that time I wouldn't be considered a resident of either North Carolina or Georgia as far as the schools I attended were concerned. The residency requirement states that a student must be a resident of the state where attending for at least one year. Tuition for a resident is a mere pittance in comparison with what out-of-state students pay. This bureaucratic nonsense infuriated me. Perhaps it was even unconstitutional. How could they mandate that a United States citizen wasn't a resident of any state?

I spoke to several people in registration, never receiving a reasonable solution to my dilemma. Finally, a compassionate staff member helped solve the problem. After he listened patiently as I moaned and groaned about the ridiculous rule, he pointed out: You will remain a resident here if you keep your North Carolina Driver's License and address. If your documents specify that you live in North Carolina, you will be allowed in-state tuition when you return for the summer semester at UNC-G. So, for the next year, though I lived in Georgia, I happily remained a North Carolinian.

THE CHICKEN DANCE

Most dances appeal to me, but I detest the Chicken Dance. The inane choreography, resembling a chicken that's continually extending its head and flapping its wings, moves too fast. No skill required. The only aim is to provoke laughter.

My Chicken Dance years. In retrospect, that's how I view the time our family spent in Georgia.

Before leaving Greensboro, I'd convinced myself that the move would be good for all of us. Atlanta is only a short distance from Marietta where we'd be living. I imagined myself driving into the big city to see plays and leisurely meandering through art galleries. Why Atlanta even had a first class opera company. I would also be able to take my son Mike to see the Braves play baseball, and we could walk through the city's beautiful greenways. Best of all, I could spend time with my brother Mick. He lived right in the middle of the city, near Peachtree Street.

The reality: My husband was responsible for a group of factory outlets scattered over four states. He left every Monday morning, returning late on Thursdays. Fridays, he spent in the

Marietta office. During the week I was busy struggling to complete my education, looking for a part-time job, and doing my best to convince my son that he would soon adjust to our new home. As for driving into Atlanta to do anything, now that was utter madness. Just learning my way around Marietta in my clunky green station wagon was an experience fraught with anxiety.

Those forced to drive on Atlanta's complicated beltway, where traffic sometimes stopped for hours, had to be absolutely bonkers. We actually had one Marietta neighbor who kept a bar in his car in case traffic stalled as he drove home from his job in Atlanta.

Yes, living close to Atlanta was a Chicken Dance, all right, and most of those Chicken Dance drivers had no idea where they were headed. One day snow fell. You would have thought the world had come to an end. Looking out the window, I watched five cars slide off the road and into my neighbor's front yard.

In Marietta, there were not only Chicken Dance drivers, there were actually chickens. The people who lived behind us owned at least a dozen. Curiously, at least half of them were roosters. I couldn't help but wonder if the brood's owner conducted cock fights for fun and profit. At least we didn't need to worry about those clucking, defecating chickens visiting our backyard. When we'd moved from North Carolina, we brought Ollie, our big black dog. Since a puppy, Ollie had been our youngest son's companion, and though the dog obviously had a personality disorder that surfaced when confronted by strangers, we forgave him. While living in Georgia. I actually valued the dog's surliness, placing my faith in his mean streak to discourage unwanted intruders.

Greensboro was, I realized, a genteel city, especially when contrasted to Cobb County where we lived in Georgia. Though we officially lived inside the city limits of Marietta and paid taxes there, the post office insisted that our mailing address be Kennesaw.

During our second year as Georgians, Kennesaw adopted an odd town ordinance (I swear this is true), stating that everyone living there had to own a handgun. One weekend, a week or so later, my husband returned from work carrying a paper bag. In a serious voice, he announced, "Well, Sandra, guess we have to comply with the ordinance. I bought us guns."

A peacenik from the top of my head to my tippy toes, I was completely speechless. Not only was Kennesaw crazy, I thought, now my husband had also caught chicken-brain disease.

Grabbing the paper bag, I looked inside. As I emptied the contents on the kitchen table, I laughed. I kept the pink water pistol, and handed the green one to my husband. Rushing to the kitchen sink, I filled mine with water first.

Marietta and Kennesaw (we never figured out where we lived) did have some perks. A small picturesque mountain, located in the Kennesaw National Battlefield Park, provided my family with respites of contentment, despite its bloody history. During the Civil War, Sherman began his Atlanta campaign on Kennesaw Mountain. His army killed or captured more than 67,000 men there. A serene spot, the mountain, with only a 700 foot incline, takes less than an hour to hike. I loved writing home to friends and family: "This morning I hiked to the top of Kennesaw Mountain." I never confessed that the trail was only slightly more than a mile.

Living near my brother Mick would, I believed, provide some compensation for no longer being near to my parents and my eldest son and his family in North Carolina.

In the past, during the few times I'd visited my brother, he'd taken great pride in showing me his city. The two of us were joined at the hip when it came to the arts; we loved debating the merits of an art exhibit or dramatic performance with one another. So, soon after the three of us, my husband, my son, and I, settled into our Marietta (or Kennesaw) home, I telephoned my brother, telling him we'd come to visit the following weekend.

Soon as I saw Mick, I realized the toll that Spondylitis, a rare genetic form of arthritis, had taken on his body and spirit. During the weeks that followed, I learned that he barely had the energy to continue working. Suffering a great deal of pain, he required many hours of bed rest and took a hand full of prescribed medications to make it through the day. At the time, he searched titles for a group of attorneys, a job that involved a great deal of driving. Because his spine had become practically immobile, making it impossible to move his neck, he worried that when it came time to renew his driver's license, he wouldn't pass the requirements.

I felt guilty that I hadn't realized how ill he'd become. Sometimes, clutching at a St. Christopher medal a Catholic friend had provided to protect me from Atlanta drivers, I'd venture out, driving down to see my brother, carrying a basket of food and books I thought he might enjoy. But during my time in Georgia, I rarely went anywhere with my brother. He simply wasn't up to it. Still we enjoyed occasional long conversations involving family, politics, history, or books we'd read. I was always Ms. Optimism and Mick, with good reason, was Mr.

Pessimism. From the battle of these two opposing views, I like to believe, we each stumbled onto occasional pebbles of truth.

Once, Mick, bless his heart, did treat me to a performance of the Atlanta Opera, a magical afternoon I'll always remember.

Fortunately, wherever I've lived, there's always been at least one good neighbor. In Marietta (or Kennesaw), the young woman, living to the left of us, was always cordial and interesting to talk to. Her husband taught at a small college in the Atlanta area, while she remained home with her two young children. She loved to read and so we often talked about favorite books. One weekend, her husband brought home a pipe organ and over the next week, installed it in their home. I enjoyed being outside, listening to the powerful music he played on Sunday afternoons. Sometimes Ollie, our big black dog, joined in, yelping and howling, and occasionally I'd also hear the faint *cluck cluck* of chickens.

Mary, a gregarious woman who worked in the branch library closest to us, also befriended me. Soon as she found out I was from North Carolina, she began singing the praises of Lee Smith, one of North Carolina's finest contemporary writers. When I confessed I'd never read anything by Lee Smith, she insisted that situation be corrected immediately. Excusing herself, she returned in a few minutes with an arm full of books, all by Lee Smith, and checked them out for me. From then on, I never went to the branch searching for books; my new friend always had recommendations waiting, and she was always right. Not only were our reading tastes similar, both of us fancied we intuitively understood William Faulkner.

Another favor Mary provided was introducing me to the

writing of Mary Hood, a woman who lived in Woodstock, a small rural town only a short distance from Marietta (or Kennesaw). I was awestruck when I read the manuscript copy of one of Mary Hood's early short stories. She hadn't yet been published, but my librarian friend and I both knew she would be. She understood Southerners at least as well as Flannery O'Connor and her prose never missed a beat. Since that conversation with the astute librarian, Mary Hood has published two fine short story collections and a novel. She's also the recipient of several writing awards. She possesses other artistic talents. I once viewed an exhibit of her paintings, which included water color scenes on hand saws and pastel portraits of dog heads. I once read that hunters in Woodstock loved her. Whenever a favorite hunting dog died, the owner would go for Mary, begging her to paint a last portrait of their beloved animal.

I'm still deeply grateful for the friendship of my neighbor and the librarian and for being introduced early on to the incredible writing of Mary Hood, a woman I still hope to personally meet someday.

Shameful as it is to admit, I, myself, turned chicken while in Georgia. Unlike the manic dance performed by kids, with arms flapping up and down, my Chicken Dance was a retreat into fear, closing myself completely off from my surroundings. I wrote letters to Greensboro friends. I read and even reviewed books by North Carolina authors for the *Atlanta Journal Constitution*. I searched the newspaper and television screen, hoping to retrieve information about North Carolina. Whenever I could avoid doing so, I didn't leave the house. Even going for groceries became traumatic. If I'd been shopping in Greensboro, I'd see familiar faces. In Marietta (or Kennesaw), I could shop all day and never see a single soul I knew. Besides my home, Kennesaw College and the neighborhood library remained the only safe sanctuaries.

Eventually my son Michael helped me adjust to Georgia. Not yet old enough to drive, I had to take him to visit friends and later, when he became a lifeguard, I chauffeured him to the two pools in Marietta where he worked. We also saved the labels from Dooley Dogs, a popular brand of hot dogs. Widely publicized on TV, we knew that if we saved enough Dooley Dog labels, we could receive free tickets to a Braves Baseball game. When we succeeded, Michael and I *bravely* set out for the big city. Though we enjoyed the game, we both became frustrated when I lost my way getting back to Marietta (or Kennesaw).

The one time my parents visited while we lived in Georgia, my husband treated them to an Atlanta Braves Play-off Game. Unfortunately the Braves lost.

Finally, after returning to study during a short summer session at UNC-G, I received my diploma for a B.A. degree in English through the mail. Watching our nickels and dimes, I considered it an unnecessary extravagance to travel home to receive the piece of paper in a formal ceremony. Still I was totally proud of the Magna cum laude embossed on my diploma.

I wrote quite a bit during our remaining years in Georgia. In addition to book reviews in the *Atlanta Journal Constitution*, I had a few short stories and poems published in journals and I won the Kennesaw College student writing award during the year I attended classes there.

During my remaining two years in Georgia, I also did substitute teaching at the high school my son attended and also at Lassiter High School. While there, I learned how mportant football is in Georgia. Some of the members of the high school teams shaved their heads in the fall. Emotions ran high as competitions between the schools began. Some times arguments over a game would erupt in the cafeteria. I was taught by one of the teachers to always keep a glass of water handy. If one student jumped another, the teachers would throw water at them. At home, if Ollie howled at night, I tried the same remedy on him, and it always worked. Mean dogs and young football players have much in common.

I sometimes tutored college students while living in Marietta (or Kennesaw). Kennesaw College would refer students to me and I'd meet with them in the college library. Two of the students I tutored, I'll never forget. One, was a man from Yemen. New to this country, he buckled at many of the rules. On the day I was to meet him at the library, I walked toward our appointed meeting spot. Even before opening the door, I smelled smoke. There, my student sat, puffing away. "I'm sorry, you'll have to get rid of the cigarette," I told him. "Smoking isn't allowed in the library."

"In my country," he replied, "women don't tell men what to do." Then he took another puff and blew smoke in my face.

After I told him he'd need to find another tutor, I left.

The most interesting person I ever tutored was a young woman who called me "Kiddo." Petite and curvaceous, her pale blonde hair cascaded about her shoulders. She always wore short shorts and espadrilles. After a couple of sessions we got into a grove. We'd work on English grammar for thirty minutes and then she'd take a talking break, which she willingly paid for. During the talking break, she shared bits and pieces of her history.

One day she told me she worked as a cook on a yacht that belonged to Ted Turner. Whenever Ted went sailing, she said she had to go along. This meant that she sometimes missed classes.

Another time, soon after our session began, she said, "Kiddo, I need to be at home. I'm expecting an important phone call. Why don't you follow me to my house and we'll finish the tutoring there?"

I gave her the look, the one that says without saying, "Are you some kind of chicken head?"

She said, "Tell you what, follow me to my house and I'll pay you double time."

Greed is one of my sins.

The young women who called me Kiddo lived in a lovely apartment, decorated primarily in black and white. A large safe took up a great deal of space in her dining room. Almost as soon as we entered, she spun the combination, opening it. Inside, I saw a large gray metal box and a hand gun. On top of the metal box she placed her pink purse before closing the door.

After she fixed us mugs of herbal tea, we sat down at a glass table and worked on verb agreement. After we finished the session, she opened the safe again and paid me. Then she asked if I'd like to see the rest of her place. "Sure," I said.

The main feature of her bedroom was a huge glass aquarium containing a boa constrictor. As a writer, I should have been able to put all the pieces together. I'm still working on it.

After my five year struggle of getting used to the weirdness of Georgia, my husband was transferred back to Greensboro. When we left, I felt a small tug of regret. I'd almost gotten use to Marietta (or Kennesaw).

Skip To My Lou

My husband's company transferred him back to Greensboro in 1984. When he told me, I wanted to jump over the moon. A childhood song I'd danced to kept tripping through my mind: *Fly's in the buttermilk/ shoo, fly, shoo/ Skip to my Lou, my darlin'*. I've never known exactly what the ditty meant, but somehow the words fit my situation. Some of my Georgia experiences had been as irritating as flies in buttermilk.

At the top of my list, when I returned to Greensboro, would be spending more time with my eldest son, his wife Pat, and their two young sons: Ben, born after we'd been in Georgia only a year, and the youngest, Dave, still a toddler. They'd visited us twice and we'd visited them during trips back to Greensboro. Once, when Dave was only six weeks old, I'd spent a week taking care of him and his brother when their mother had been hospitalized for emergency gall bladder surgery. My arms ached to hold both boys once more.

While in Georgia, I'd battled agoraphobia and bronchitis. I blamed the isolation. I blamed the lushness of the landscape. I blamed flies in buttermilk. Back then I believed that returning to Greensboro would change everything. Now, in retrospect, I realize that failing to make the most of living in Marietta (or Kennesaw) had been my own fault.

Immediately, I breezed about, happily making preparations for the move. On the following Saturday, we steamed crab legs and corn on the cob. We even opened a bottle of wine to celebrate. My husband, like me, looked forward to being in Greensboro again. His promotion would bring new opportunities and his work schedule wouldn't involve so much traveling. But not everyone was pleased. As we ate, I noticed the corners of Michael's mouth turn down. Joe and I were laughing, but my son looked as if he'd been bitten by a bug.

Of course, he'd be unhappy. Unlike me, he made lots of friends in Marietta. This had become his world. Because he'd lost touch with the buddies in Greensboro, he'd have to start over. My heart ached for him. He was now feeling the way I'd felt when we'd moved to Georgia. "Mike," I said, "Trust me; it's going to be okay."

"For you, maybe," he answered.

Soon as we settled into Hamilton Village, a condominium community near Guilford College in Greensboro, I began visiting the former haunts I loved—the public library in downtown Greensboro, Weatherspoon Art Gallery at UNC-G, and Atticus Book Store. On Saturday mornings, I looked forward to getting up before the sun rose and heading out for the Farmer's Curb Market located on Yanceyville Street. Walking around and talking to those who had stalls filled with incredible flowers and fresh veggies was a real treat then. It still is today. A favorite purchase in summer has always been juicy German Johnson tomatoes. And nothing quite compares to the scent of fresh peaches or later, in August, to the scent of muscadines.

Before leaving, I always headed for one of the flower stalls. Usually I purchased at least one bunch. Sometimes I'd choose the fragrant tuberoses, another time a mixed bouquet containing zinnias, lilies, and Queen Anne's lace. Sometimes I'd even select sunflowers. Then I'd take the blooms home and, after carefully arranging them in vases, I'd place a bouquet in the dining room and another in the living room. The sweetness of flowers became my inspiration, spurring me on to clean up the house. Once, when we were placed in charge of the Redding Reunion, attended by over sixty of my husband's relatives, I purchased an armload of flowers from the farmer's market, enough to have a canning jar full of them centering each table.

Across the street from the farmers market stands the Memorial Ball Stadium. My family always enjoyed going there on summer evening to watch the Bats baseball team. Though it lacked the bells and whistles found at Greensboro's new Horizon Park Stadium, it definitely had charm. And the hotdogs were even tastier than those served at Yum-Yums on Spring Garden Street.

Nancy and Bill Poe, friends since high school, welcomed us back to Greensboro. And my husband had colleagues from work who invited us out. A special reunion for me was meeting with favorite Greensboro writers again.

One of them, generous Evelyn Gill, always took the time to read and praise my short stories. Founding editor of the *International Poetry Review* and the author of several poetry collections, her stories appeared in *Crucible* and other area publications. She eventually spearheaded the formation of the Triad Writers group, a gathering of women who encouraged one another. With her support, the group published several anthologies over the years. I felt fortunate that my work appeared in them, along with other emerging writers, including Susan Kelly, Mary Elizabeth Parker, Marsha Van Hecke, and Alice Owens Johnson. I admired Evelyn tremendously for the beauty of her own writing and for the generosity she extended to other dedicated poets and prose writers.

Another valuable friend who encouraged me even before the callus on my writing finger hardened was Marie Gilbert. Marie, born in Florida, and her husband Richard lived in several places before settling in Greensboro. Her presence brought a bright light to our city. A tall genteel woman, her hair already gray the first time I met her, she embodied Southern grace. At our first meeting, I warmed to her. In a soft unimposing voice, she told us she enjoyed reading and writing poetry. Within a few years, Marie published several books of poems, and the North Carolina writing community embraced her.

In addition to our connection as writers, I had another reason for admiring her. Though she owned three impressive homes, one in Greensboro, one at DeBordieu, a gated community on the coast of South Carolina, and a citrus orchard in Florida, Marie was one of the thriftiest people I've ever known. She embraced sustainability, even before it became popular to do so. Though she lived at least two miles from me, she'd often walk to my house rather than drive over. After returning from a trip to her Florida orchard, she'd bring me beautiful oranges and grapefruits in a plastic bag. Before leaving, she'd ask softly, would you mind giving the plastic bag back?

I also learned tips on how to stay fit from Marie. She had the straightest back of anyone I knew over the age of sixty. Once, while in her Greensboro home, she pointed out the bars fastened near the tops of the doorways. When she passed from one room to another, she'd stop, lift her arms, and grasp the bar for a minute or so. And when at her home in DeBordieu, she swam each day in the ocean.

One of the best times we shared was at Weymouth, a retreat for writers in Southern Pines. We were invited to spend a week there writing. Most of the day, we remained in our rooms, pleading for our muses to help us get our story or poem onto the page.

At 1:00 each day, we'd break for lunch. Marie, always thrifty with time as well as money, brought the makings for quiche with her, so the first day that's what we ate, quiche accompanied by tossed salads. The second day, Marie said, we still have quiche, so that's what we ate again. The third day, when she offered more quiche, I rolled my eyes and smiled. "Thanks, Marie, but I'm all quiched out."

She thought that was terrible funny. When she stopped giggling, I confessed, "I need a fast food fix. Why don't we find a McDonald's or Burger King?

"I've never been to a fast food restaurant," Marie confessed.

"Well, then," I countered, "It's about time."

We ended up at Burger King. Marie had little to say about the food, but she was intrigued with the free Burger King hats they gave to children. Before we left, she asked the waitress if she could have a few of them, so she could play "fast food restaurant" with her grandchildren.

While we were at Weymouth, Steve Smith, a talented local

writer and musician came by. Sam Ragan also visited us. Sam, former Poet Laureate of North Carolina, was responsible for the restoration of Weymouth so that it could be a place where writers could congregate. James Boyd, author and an early editor of the *Southern Pines* newspaper, originally owned the house. Scott and Zelda Fitzgerald and Thomas Wolfe were only a few of the celebrated authors staying there during Boyd's lifetime. Autographed books of North Carolina's greatest writers rest on the shelves there. And outside, the surrounding yard and gardens remain spectacular, the scent of pine always fragrancing the air.

When I confessed to Sam that, thus far, my muse had been lollygagging during my stay, a magnanimous grin spread across his kind face. Weymouth wasn't intended just for writing, he reminded me. Sometimes writers needed to do nothing but be quiet and contemplate their surroundings. When we least expect it, he explained, that's when creative juices flow.

After he left that afternoon, my muse must have returned. I began and completed a short story. Was it the magic or Weymouth or the magic of Sam?

Marie, like me, loved Greensboro, but a few years ago she left to live near St. Andrews Presbyterian College in Laurinburg, North Carolina. When I saw her in the summer of 2007 at the North Carolina Writer's Conference held in Hillsborough, she confessed she missed Greensboro. Greensboro certainly missed her.

In November of 2007, Marie died after a stroke. Still often she seems to be nearby, reminding me to walk every day and to believe that what I write is important.

The third writer who influenced me early-on was Ann Deagon.

Unlike Evelyn and Marie, Ann is still on this earth, and most definitely alive. Indeed she remains a life force that grows more vibrant each time I talk to her. Possessing the spirit of a Renaissance woman, Ann delves into many arts. Her publications include two books of poetry, a collection of short stories, and a novel. She also loves acting. Once, she and her husband Donald spent summers in the North Carolina mountains, performing in the outdoor drama, *Unto These Hills*. Anne has also frequently performed in area plays and has been an extra in several films produced in the state. A singer, she's entertained locally and abroad. Sometimes she writes songs. A popular favorite of mine is a ballad about Nero fiddling as Rome burns.

Before retiring, Ann taught classics at Guilford College. That's where I first met her. We were both members of the North Carolina Poetry Society. Another member of that organization, John Pipkin, who taught religion at Guilford for many years, would invite some of the Greensboro members of the society to his office on Sunday afternoons to read and talk about poetry. Ann was usually there.

Later she formed a group for Greensboro writers. How I loved those meetings, held in an upstairs room of the Guilford College campus library. Somehow, Ann lured phenomenal writers from across North Carolina to talk to us or read from their books. Often, after the meeting, she would invite us to drop by her house. In those days she frequented yard sales, so it was always a delight to see what new treasure she had procured. My favorite was the suit of armor standing in her living room. Of course, there were many other treasures, some from her travels to Greece. We would laugh and talk about writing or anything else that might occur to us.

I remember once, as we were drinking some of the beer that her husband had brewed prior to his death, she announced that we were having the last of Donald's beer. I felt such a strange mixture of happiness and sadness. I hated that Greensboro, Guilford College, and, particularly, my friend Ann had lost such a special person, but mixed with the sorrow was joy, for he had died still living pretty much on his own terms.

Today Ann has a new partner, a talented musician. I know only a few others who derive such satisfaction from life. She's certainly a talented artist, but I believe that to be secondary to an even greater mission: I've known only a few others who have embraced life with such gusto.

Nancy Gates is another valued writing cohort I met through that early writer's group. Nancy wrote poetry then and was also a gifted visual artist. Always dedicated and persistent, she worked on several impressive group writing projects. Now a mystery writer, she's published three books in that genre. Her sweet helpful demeanor might seem out of place for someone who enjoys writing of people dying mysteriously, but that interest, I believe, has developed from a curiosity that keeps her interested in both people and places.

CAN YOU DANCE?

After reconnecting with Greensboro friends, I settled down to some serious soul searching. While in Atlanta, I'd blamed the rough ride on where I lived. Now, back in the city I'd deemed *home, sweet home*, I had to face the music. Looking into the mirror one morning, I said, "Well, old girl, it's time to find out if you can dance." By dance, I didn't mean a series of programmed steps to music. What I needed was to find a new rhythm, a confidence that would glide me through both the good times and the bad. No more agoraphobic retreating, I promised myself. Confess what you really want, then go for it.

Gradually my mirror conversations took hold, but not at first.

During that first year back in Greensboro, I worried a great deal about my son Mike. Gregarious and friendly, he always made friends easily, but fitting into a new school when you're a junior is no easy task. High school years are difficult enough for young people without having to be the new kid in town. Still, the next year, when he marched up in cap and gown to receive his diploma from Western Guilford High School was a stellar moment for our entire family.

Michael enjoyed working more than going to classes. While attending school, he'd always had part-time jobs, as a lifeguard during the summer and working for a grocery store during the school year. After high school he attended Guilford Technical Community College, but working always remained a priority. Unlike his mother, he had too much energy to sit for hours with a book in front of his nose. As long as he had a job that gave him a chance to interact with other people, he thrived. That's never changed. Today he's a successful real estate agent in Myrtle Beach, cheerfully helping other people realize their dream of purchasing or selling a home.

Within a year after graduating from high school, Michael took a job with a Kernersville car dealership and moved out, into an apartment of his own. For a while, missing his laughter and the quirky stories he told about people he knew, I actually ached. In an attempt to hold onto some part of him, I'd sometimes put on a flannel shirt he'd left behind. Sniffing the sleeve, I inhaled my son's essence, as I recalled the joy he always brought to my husband and me.

Eventually, after nearly a month of wallowing in empty nest woes, I put the shirt in a bag of clothes intended for Goodwill and resumed my mirror sessions. *Time to decide what to do next, old girl. Time to learn a new dance.*

For a few years after returning to Greensboro, I worked for Pennsylvania National Insurance Company. I eventually became their computer troubleshooter, a strange job indeed, for I had practically no computer expertise. At that time the purpose of the computer operation where I worked was to interact with the home office. Sometimes I received calls from frantic employees, claiming the computer wasn't working. Sometimes, just asking if they'd remembered to turn it on solved the problem.

One morning an employee informed me that her keyboard wouldn't work. She explained that it should be operating *super good*, because before leaving work the previous afternoon, she'd cleaned it.

"Exactly how did you clean it?" I asked.

With Windex was her reply.

After patiently explaining that electronics and water-based cleansers weren't compatible, I found her a new keyboard.

Besides the trouble-shooting, I also typed contracts, not a cup of comfort. But another part of my job description was helping with a newsletter, definitely a cup of joy. After more talks to the mirror, reminding myself how much I loved putting words on paper, I finally, after months of agonizing, decided to apply for the Master of Fine Arts in Creative Writing Program offered by the University of North Carolina in my home town. In mirror talks I prepared myself for rejection, but finally met with Jim Clark, coordinator of the program, for advice.

Jim explained that the most important component was the required writing sample. Although prospective students could submit both poetry and prose, he advised that I submit prose only. That suited me. Though I had published a good bit of poetry, I realized then and now that my writing strength is the ability to tell a story.

It must be in my genes. My mother, though she never attempted to write anything except a diary and long interesting letters, told phenomenal stories. Her dramatic recitations always began with fact, but by the conclusion drifted off into fiction due to her heavy reliance on speculation. For example, in her story of an uncle who disappeared, leaving his wife and children, the clincher was how at family funerals, the wife and children always showed up and sat at the back of the room, looking around to see if Uncle Gage might be there.

So, keeping Jim's advice in mind, I submitted copies of a couple of my quirky stories, neither as compelling as my mother's oral renditions. Within a few weeks I received a letter notifying me that I'd been accepted. Initially, I was so overjoyed, I felt as if I might pop right open, but then anxiety grabbed hold. I hadn't told any one about applying. What would my husband say? What about my job?

Foolishly I kept my acceptance into the program a secret for nearly a week. Finally I attempted to explain to my husband, "This is something I really want. In four years I'll be fifty, so if I don't do it now, I probably never will."

Though it would be a sacrifice for both of us, he agreed that I should go ahead. The next day, when I explained to my employer, noting that I'd have to leave work early two days a week for classes, but would be willing to make up any lost time, even working on Saturdays, I was asked, "What if the company says no?"

"Then I'll have to quit," was my reply.

They agreed but within a year, the Greensboro office of Pennsylvania National was instructed by the home office to lay off a large number of people. My name was on the dismissal list.

Anxious to spend more time writing and completing the work for my M.F.A., I didn't mind having to leave the job, but there were people I knew I'd miss. At the top of the list was Bill Mullins.

During my first year at Pennsylvania National, Bill had been my supervisor. Fond of telling stories, he engaged the interest of all of us with the engaging knowledge floating about in his brain.

Though Bill left Pennsylvania National many years ago, he still sells insurance. Also a beekeeper, he sells honey, his wife's delectable cakes, and yummy summer tomatoes at the Greensboro Curb Market on Yanceyville Street. Like the Eveready bunny, he keeps going and going. Still, I think Bill's biggest delight is simply talking and listening to people. Because he's a person with dreams and the ability to see them through, I've long admired him.

The Varsity Rag

When I received my B.A. in English, I knew I'd just begun. My appetite for facts and connections and a proclivity to question absolutely everything had only been whetted by that experience. My need for learning more would never be sated. I'd feared that continuing my education would be a lonely Lincolnesque experience. Like poor Abe I'd have to slog through books on my own. That, I knew, would be a problem, for my brain is too scattered to maintain focus for long periods of time. So, with my acceptance into the M.F.A. program at the University of North Carolina in Greensboro, I believed I had landed on a magic carpet that would carry me through a universe of wisdom and knowing. Surely everything I needed to know to be a writer would be revealed.

Ha! I should have been concentrating on everything I needed to know to about people. That, after all, is life's central issue and well-written fiction flows out of whatever small stream of knowledge one is lucky enough to acquire concerning human nature.

In my head I was a princess being led by a unicorn when I returned to campus that first day. That's how ridiculously out of touch I'd become. I walked around, inanely touching the outside wall of McIver Hall, the revered building where as an undergraduate I'd studied Shakespeare, Chaucer, Dickinson. The place where I'd had the privilege of penning a few simple-minded poems and turning in essays that received A's either for scholarship or sassiness. I was never quite sure which.

Then I walked over to Jackson Library, which had been my sanctuary while working on my B.A. in English. The pensive portrait of Randall Jarrell still hung on the wall. I could take an elevator up to the stacks, sit down at a table, and pretend some of the knowledge in those books could miraculously sink into my own thick skull. After leaving the library I passed "Charlie", a statue of he University's founder Charles Duncan McIver. He wore a Hawaiian lei that day. Red freckles spotted his somber face. Poor Charlie. Exuberant students had their way with him then. Students today are no longer allowed to abuse him by adding paint and clothing.

Heading for Elliott University Student Center to purchase some small notebooks in the bookstore, I stopped and smiled at the inane message for a pajama party written on The Rawk, a large boulder that has been on campus since the 1970's. Students are allowed to spray paint a message on The Rawk, but the message must stay at least 24 hours before being changed. No need to abuse the Rawk too frequently.

Once inside the bookstore, I was disappointed when I discovered that images of the male Spartan mascot were imprinted on many items. Originally the logo contained the profile of a female Spartan, but later, the campus became co-ed.

In an effort to attract more men, the logo was changed. Though Minerva, the female mascot remains, the male Spartan warrior gets top billing. That day, unable to find notebooks with Minerva printed on the front, I decided to purchase my notebooks at Wall-Mart instead.

My next stop was the Weatherspoon Art Gallery to view the art currently gracing the walls, and then off to Yum-Yums for ice cream.

One of the oldest most respected writing programs in the United States, the MFA Creative Writing program at UNCG began in 1965 under the leadership of Robert Watson. Though the years the program has been kept small so that students could meet for conferences with the faculty. When I was accepted in the program, Jim Clark was coordinator and Fred Chappell was the school's most celebrated instructor. Beloved throughout the country, he has published over a dozen books. A North Carolina Poet Laureate emeritus, Fred has now retired from teaching.

I don't specifically know what I expected, but the first day in the fiction workshop taught by Fred held surprises. First, before the class began, he walked into the room and wrote a quote on the board, then left. I can't recall the quote. I only remember thinking, well if Fred Chappell wrote it, it must be important. I still don't know whether those words were intended to change my life or just confound me. The quotes continued throughout the semester with no explanation. I never asked about them. I was too awe-struck at being in a class taught by Fred. If he wrote it, it must be valuable, so I simply wrote each one down to study later.

There was little conversation among students that first day

until Fred walked back into the room. Fred suggested that each of us tell a bit about ourselves. One scruffy young male student announced that he'd been in jail and had feared that he wouldn't be released in time to make his classes.

Fred had some comeback that made everyone else laugh, but I didn't. My chest hurt, as if an icicle had touched my heart. It's a cold odd sensation I've had from time to time. A warning. Sometimes walking by myself in the evening I have a similar feeling. Whenever that happens, I always cross the street and walk on the opposite side.

Though I love classrooms, particularly when a wise teacher leads an interesting discourse, being shut up in a room with total strangers can be claustrophobic. Still, once we got down to reading and discussing stories, I relaxed. Our instructions were to go by the library prior to each class and request copies of the stories to be discussed. We read the manuscripts before class, and then, when we met again, we critiqued the stories orally. When I critiqued, I wanted to be kind and helpful. Perhaps as much as anything, a writer needs encouragement, but I also felt an obligation to detail what, in my opinion, didn't work. Wasn't that what I wished from others when my own writing was discussed?

Many positives came out of these critique sessions. I discovered not only flaws in my stories but also in myself through comments made by other students. The truth about writing fiction is that even when you write a story about a person totally different from yourself, it's your own blood and guts that cling to the page. Each sentence uncovers your feelings and exposes biases.

Fred Chappell, though his methods didn't always make sense to me, was a superb teacher. He understood how stories worked.

More important, a heart-and-soul poet, he appreciated language. Words, to him, were remarkable gems and he knew how to string them together into memorable passages. In his fiction workshop, he occasionally went slightly berserk when words were used incorrectly. I recall that someone once wrote of celery ribs, meaning a celery stalk. Fred mentioned the error, explaining in great detail exactly what a celery rib was. He looked as if our ignorance caused him great pain. Sometimes I wondered why he made such a big deal about word usage, but the more I wrote the more I appreciated his desire for preciseness. Later, when I taught writing workshops, I became almost as fanatical as Fred over students' careless misuse of language.

The truth of description also mattered deeply to Fred. In one workshop, someone submitted a short story in which the protagonist, a maid at a motel, obviously envying the easy life she believed the guests must have, reverently picked up items in the room she was cleaning, then collapsed ecstatically across the unmade bed.

Fred wryly explained that he'd once had a job cleaning rooms. In blunt terms he let us know there's nothing romantic about the trash and filth that people leave behind. He couldn't imagine anyone wanting to crawl into a motel bed that someone else had been tumbling around in.

Before I enrolled in the writing program, I'd asked a local writer who had years earlier received her MFA degree what she thought of Fred Chappell's instruction. The writer believed she'd learned a great deal from Fred but couldn't explain precisely how. Finally, she said "It's intuitive." I believe that to be accurate. You read what he's written and listen to what he says and somehow you absorb a distillation that serves your own writing. Still some of his teaching methods relied on simple logic. Once after critiquing a story of mine, he turned the manuscript over, asking me to select three pages. Then with a pencil, he went over those pages, line by line, deleting and rearranging words. Though embarrassed to discover the flabbiness of my prose, the lesson improved my editing skills considerably.

During my time in the program, I read all the books written by Fred that I hadn't previously devoured. I particularly loved his short stories and the novels, *I Am One of You Forever* and *Brighten the Corner Where You Are*.

I also felt privileged to have Robert Watson for an instructor while in the program. Bob had personally known so many writers of the twentieth century and he loved telling students about them. He told of spending time with Robert Frost who would stop at by UNC-G on the trip he made each year to spend winter in Florida. He told tales of many other famous writers, including Peter Taylor and Randall Jarrell. Peter Taylor, the celebrated Virginia writer, actually taught in the MFA Program at Woman's College (now the University of North Carolina in Greensboro) early on. Later, Randall Jarrell, noted poet, critic and translator, came to the campus to teach. Loving it there, he once called the campus, "A sleeping beauty," connoting that its splendor and also its potential had not yet been recognized. Of course, today, with the physical growth and academic advancement of the campus, the school has received a great deal of recognition. Over 16,000 students are enrolled and the University has, in recent years, excelled at research.

I was actually in Bob Watson's class the last semester he taught at the University. His wife Betty, a well-loved, artist, also taught there.

In the workshop sessions, besides sharing amusing stories about other writers, he would gently point out what worked and what didn't in a piece of writing. Then he would give us our turn to dissect and reprimand.

Near the end of the semester, Bob entertained students in his home. On the coffee table in the living room, he'd placed an anthology containing a short story I'd written. During the evening, he mentioned my story, and before I left, he congratulated me and pointed out what he believed to be the story's merits. Though immensely pleased, I wasn't surprised. Of all writers I've known, he possessed the most generous spirit.

Though no one has ever suggested (at least to my face) that I'm schizophrenic, there is a rascal inside of me. Sometimes, when aggravated by a word or act of another person, the monster pops out. It happened at least three times while I studied for my M.F.A.

I believe it's assumed that if you're in the creative writing program you'll make all A's. I became an exception. I could have had all A's but that stubborn woolly booger who's haunted me since childhood threw a wrench in those plans.

One of the graduate English courses I took required a paper comparing two writers. The professor of the course will go unnamed to protect the innocent (maybe, though I have never been convinced of his innocence). The deal with the paper was that each person in the class would decide on a topic, have a conference with the professor, and once approval was granted, get the paper written.

I loved research, so before making my decision I scoured many books in the cozy stacks of the library. Finally I made my decision, coming up with two authors, both well known in

England, but less well-known in the United States. I made my appointment with the professor and presented the argument for the topic I'd selected. He agreed and we shook hands.

I remember even now the relief that washed over me. Wanting to get ahead of the game by finishing the paper as soon as possible, I headed back to the library when our conference ended. I spent the afternoon reading and making notes. By the time of my next class with that particular professor, I'd spent over fifteen hours researching and making notes.

At the conclusion of the next class, the professor said he'd like to see me. Even today, remembering his words, I'm astonished. The gist was that he'd been thinking about the topic I'd chosen and had come to the conclusion that it wouldn't do. I believe it was that one of the writers wasn't important enough.

"But you okayed it," I reminded him. "I've already begun."

He appeared quite unconcerned. He had simply changed his mind; I would have to accept his decision.

The ugly rascal inside of me wiggled free and it was all I could do to keep from hitting that damned professor over the head with my textbook. "What if I write the paper anyway?" I asked. "I don't have time to come up with a new topic. I've been concentrating on finishing this one so that I can get back to writing stories," I said, reminding him that learning all I could about writing fiction remained my main goal.

Throwing down the gauntlet, he informed me that to make an A in the course, I'd have to write about something else."

Becoming even more pig-headed, I assured him that though I worked for and expected A's, not making one wouldn't hurt nearly as much as not doing what I believed to be right.

After that, we spoke of it no more. I remember studying

very hard for the final exam and did make an A on it. I also worked very hard on the paper I wrote for the class. He gave me a B-.

At the end of the semester, I found that my final grade for the course was B+. Though I knew I wouldn't be making an A, the B+ infuriated me. I didn't even know the university gave B pluses. I'd never before had a plus or minus added to a grade I received there. I suppose he wanted to reiterate that I would have gotten an A if I'd walked the line he drew. Still I've never regretted the stand I took. Though I've always been intrigued with the Eastern notion of "bend as the bamboo" or temporarily accepting a situation that annoys one, I've never been good at *bending*. Once, as a child, a neighborhood kid bent my thumb back further and further, demanding that I say, "Uncle". Finally, in a great deal of pain and fearing my thumb would be broken, I pretended to pass out. That scared the be-Jesus out of the bully, and he ran away. I wish, during my confrontation with the adamant professor, I'd tried the same trick.

Another encounter that I found upsetting was with the young man who revealed he'd just gotten out of jail the first day of Fred Chappell's workshop. There is the type of writer, usually young but not always, and usually male, but not always, who muscles his or her way through, believing that being a "writer" entitles them to bad behavior. Sometimes, "I've had a difficult childhood" receives the blame or "alcohol or drugs" may be the excuse given. Sometimes it's simply because I'm so brilliant (in the person's own opinion, not necessarily anyone else's) the usual rules don't apply. This particular young man, at a public function honoring Bob Watson, flashed me and several others. He exited the men's bathroom as I stood talking to a group in the hallway. He opened the long coat he wore, shocking us. His excuse later, was that he'd been drinking and remembered nothing about it. That was just one instance of his sophomoric conduct. On several other occasions, he behaved raucoulsly at university events. Though he was not the only bad boy or girl I encountered during my time in the writing program, he took the Oscar. When I complained about his behavior, I suggested that since he apparently didn't know how to behave at public functions, perhaps he should be prevented from attending them. I was informed that would violate his rights. I didn't pursue the matter, for fear, I suppose, that I might be kicking a dent into the future career of a literary genius.

While working for my MFA in Creative Writing, the age difference was a problem. Perhaps if I'd baked cookies and taken them to class and told everyone their stories were "awesome", my crow's feet would have been forgiven. But I wore jeans just as they did. I also expressed opinions. Still over half the class treated me with equality despite the age difference.

One semester Jim Clark, Coordinator of the writing program, told me that he'd invited Mary Hood to be the visiting writer during the spring semester. Thrilled with the news, I looked forward to her visit, imagining that the two of us would have long interesting conversations about writing. I'd known of Mary, while living in Georgia, and through reading her work I felt a connection. During the years since I'd returned to North Carolina, her fiction had been received and celebrated by the literary community.

Later Jim told me that because Mary's father was ill, she wouldn't be able to come. A dull ache of disappointment lingered inside me for several days.

Despite lacking confidence, I finally earned enough credit to receive my degree. The one task left was to submit my short stories for approval. Every margin had to be just so. First my manuscript went to Fred Chappell who was my advisor. Then Jim Clark looked over the collection. With their approval, I submitted my thesis to the administrative office. Within a few days, the manuscript came sailing back with a note stating that the page numbers were inconsistent, some of them a fraction of an inch lower on the page than others.

I felt I was going absolutely nuts. How could my numbering be off? I'd left my printer at the same setting for every page. Distraught, I took my manuscript to my husband, asking his advice. Turned out there was a miniscule drift, but by copying only ten pages at the time, the numbers would appear too close to the same spot to detect a difference.

How relieved I felt when my retyped manuscript was approved. All the problems I'd confronted with getting my M.F.A. degree had been resolved. It hadn't been so difficult after all.

Then more bad news: Though I had all the necessary approvals, I'd messed up again. A paper had been tacked to the bulletin board in the English Department stating that all candidates, expecting to graduate in May, needed to fill out a form with their name printed on it, returning it to the administrative office by the end of January. It was already March.

Gee whiz, how could it be so important? Apparently, a parent had complained a few years before because their fair-haired child's name had been misspelled on the diploma. No problem, I decided. I'd be willing to sign a statement that I wouldn't object if my name were misspelled. I checked with Jim Clark. He informed me that they were unlikely to bend the rules. I decided to consult the administrative office anyway.

When I met Fred Chappell in the hallway, I explained the problem to him, and asked if he had any suggestions. Eat garlic before talking to them, he advised.

I should have taken his advice and consumed enough to drive an army away. With nary a gleam of sympathy in her cold eyes, the clerk informed me there was absolutely no way I could graduate in May.

"Maybe I'll just drop out" I threatened. "This program is driving me crazy, anyway. I'll be fifty by then. I intend to graduate before I've lived half a century."

Well, she let me know, it's your choice.

That ugly animal side emerged again. Rising from the chair, I snarled and left.

Of course, I did fill out the slip of paper. And I did graduate in August. I was terribly angry then, but I realize now it's a blessing. At this stage of my life, I might have difficulty remembering that I graduated at 49, but 50, now that's an easy-to-remember round number.

Joey and Mike's Families

Son Joey Redding and Family with pets. From left, Ben, Dave, Janet, Chais McCurry, Alice, and Joey

Son Mike Redding and Family. From Left, Tina, Amber, Mike, and Shanna

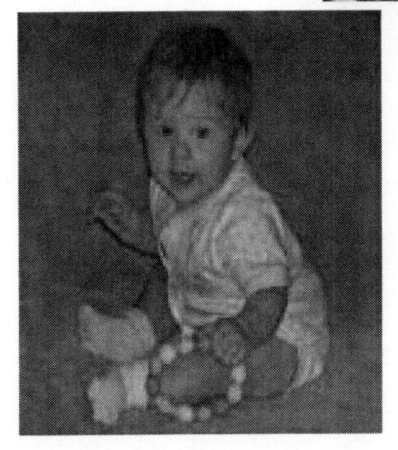

Newest edition: Granddaughter Emily Renee

Photographs courtesy of Joe, Joey, and Mike Redding

Redding Family Christmas

From left, Amber, Tina, Sandra, Ben, Joey, Dave, Mike, and Janet

Grandpop with Ben (L) and Dave

Party Time

From left, Louise Redding,
Nella Lilly,
Tina Redding, and Emily

Kittie and Lowell Schlecht

Amber and Grandpop

Ione Woodlief and Nancy Poe
admiring Elvis

Sharing My Moves

In January 1990, I began teaching creative writing classes at Guilford Technical Community College (GTCC). Writing had been the dance I'd chosen. Though I still had a great deal to learn, it was time to share the bits of wisdom I'd acquired with others.

When I entered the ancient three-story brick building on Washington Street, the downtown branch of GTCC, a wave of nostalgia washed over me. I recalled how, during the 1960's, I had come through the same door, elated that finally I would get my first taste of higher education. During the 1960's, the building had been used by Guilford College to offer students classes convenient to the bustling downtown area. My reason for signing up for courses had been to escape the hosiery mill where I worked. Hosiery mills were the backbone of the economy in Randleman then. I knew many, my father among them, who remained content working in textiles. I was not one of them. I desperately needed to find another way to earn a living. In addition to no opportunity for advancement, I was not suited to the job of hosiery inspector.

Afflicted with a mind that constantly questioned and frequently flitted into imaginative realms, I found concentrating on repetitive tasks difficult.

John King, a Randleman Pharmacist, had also enrolled in courses at the Greensboro Division of Guilford College. If he had not allowed me to ride with him, attending classes would not have been possible. I will always be grateful. He even refused payment, saying, "I have to go anyway." Since then, whenever anyone I know needs a ride, I readily agree. It's my way of paying forward Mr. King's generosity.

As soon as I began classes in accounting and speech, my mind blossomed with new possibilities. I still recall sitting in the public speaking class I took in 1960. The instructor for the course was a beautiful middle-aged woman. She wore a fur coat to class and a large diamond glittered on her left hand. Her demeanor was so confident that everyone in the class listened intently. Like a hungry bird, I digested every tidbit of knowledge she offered. One day as she offered us guidelines for speaking extemporaneously, an odd notion wiggled into my brain: perhaps I, too, could be a teacher some day.

In 1990, as I stood in the building I'd long ago attended as a student, I beamed as I realized my dream had come true. Inhaling deeply, I wondered if I had something of value to offer the students enrolled. Would I be able to gain their respect? Both exhilarated and anxious, I ascended steps to the second floor.

At the top of the stairs, I glanced out the window. Across the street, on a rolling hill, stood Blandwood, the Italianate house which had once belonged to former Governor John Motley Morehead. When I heard a train pass through the downtown area, I smiled. More than a century before, Governor Morehead had successfully campaigned for the railroad tracks to run through this city. Perhaps I owed him a big thank you. Because of those train tracks, Greensboro grew and prospered, becoming a hub offering opportunities for education as well as a wide variety of jobs to citizens.

Teaching in that building was familiar as my childhood. I loved the creaks and groans as I walked across the floor. I even liked the pine oil smell of the place. Oddly, during my years of teaching, I always preferred the old blackboards, not the new white ones. And an older desk, one made of study wood, was just right, in my opinion.

Most of my students were at least thirty years old and eager to learn. With the continuing education classes, no grades were given. Those desiring to write came to share their stories and poems with me and the other students.

With writing, as with life, there are only a few basic do's. During my years of teaching, I urged students to write whatever they felt passionate about. If they were not excited about their stories and poems, how could they expect anyone else to be? I also urged them to observe like crazy. "Notice not only how something looks, but also how it smells, feels, and moves. Use all the senses. Look for connections, look for patterns, search for meaning. And tell your own truth, whatever that might be. Offering them a simplistic approach, I suggested they write every day. The bottom line for succeeding at writing is to spend a great deal of time stringing words across the page. Another valuable aid is to read a great deal, figuring out what does and does not work.

My students were wise and smart, and over the years, I learned more from them than I could have ever provided in the instruction I offered for their enlightenment. Still it amazed me how literally my students took what I told them about writing. Well, at least most of them.

An exception was Anne Barnhill, a high school English teacher who lived in the Guilford College area of Greensboro with her husband Frank and their three sons.

Anne, then in her thirties, had dark hair and appealingly pale English skin. I admired her writing early on. I also admired her knowledge and passion for literature and her spunky personality. Anne, both then and now, had a sweet view of the world and belief under girded her opinions. She was an original. It's always those rare *originals*—people who ignore trends, deciding for themselves—who most appeal to me.

A talented writer, her contribution to the class was appreciated, but I noticed that she seemed troubled. After my last class in the six-week session, Anne hung around to talk. When we were alone, she took a deep breath before announcing, "I'm going to quit teaching, so I can write."

Oh, my God. Feeling responsible, I reminded her of what I'd said in class: *Wanna-be authors should always keep their day jobs.* Few writers support themselves solely on publications.

Despite my advice, Anne did quit teaching high school that year. Eventually, she attended the University of North Carolina at Wilmington where she received a Master's degree in writing. Over the years since, she's published many articles and book reviews and has also published a number of fine short stories and poems.

Once, along with another gifted writer, Kathryn Lovatt, Anne and I formed a critique group. Once a week, over lunch, the three of us espoused on all we knew of fiction, sharing opinions, experiences, and our stories. Though I'm the only one still living in Greensboro, the three of us still get together occasionally, usually at Kathryn's beautiful home in South Carolina. Last year, we celebrated when Anne's poignant memoir, *In the Land of Oz: My Sister, Autism and Me* was published.

Yes, Anne ignored my advice, but years later, her son Michael Smith, while taking my creative writing class, did not. Instead he took what I said too literally.

Before enrolling in a poetry class I taught, Michael had been working toward an undergraduate degree at the University of North Carolina in Greensboro. After being sick and missing several classes, he temporarily dropped out. His mother encouraged him to enroll in my course at GTCC. Handsome and young, Michael wanted to become a poet. Right away he began bringing work to read to the class. Most of my students were forty-plus women during that particular session. They treated Michael as if he were a prince, praising each lyrical line that he wrote. Like his mother, he had a gift for words. Still, I realized that there was much for him, as well as my other students, to learn.

One night, getting carried away, I pompously told the class, "If you really want to be a poet, you need to try all forms of verse. Write sonnets and villanelles. Try haiku." What I didn't reveal was that I'd actually composed only one sonnet and four haiku. Just thinking about writing a villanelle gave me a headache.

The next week Michael came to class looking as pale and languished as John Keats must have appeared prior to leaving this world. When I asked who had poems to be critiqued, Michael turned in two sonnets and a villanelle. He'd stayed up nights working on them. While the class took a fifteen minute break, I read his poems. They were extraordinary. I quickly dabbed at my eyes with a tissue before the students returned.

Michael, following a path similar to that of his mother, finished work on his English degree at UNC-G. Later he earned degrees from Hollins College and the University of Notre Dame. In recent years he has published extensively while teaching at several colleges and universities, including The University of the Americas. Earlier this year, his first book of poems, *How to Make a Mummy,* was published.

Folk Dance

During the mid-1990's I spent a great deal of time in Randleman.

My mother and father still lived in the gray house with a rock chimney and flagstone porch, the home where I'd grown up. By that time, my brother Mick lived there, too. He'd retired on disability from the Atlanta law firm where he worked. Since serving in the Air Force, he'd battled Spondylitis Angolosing, a rare genetic form of arthritis that froze his spine, eventually bending him like a boomerang, making movements of the neck or waist impossible. His knees and vision were also affected. Because of this disability, though still in his forties, he could no longer drive. Soon after moving in with Mom and Dad, he had the garage behind our parent's house converted into a small apartment, providing him with separate living space.

I loved all three of them, so it was difficult for me to witness their slow waltz toward more pain and inevitable death.

My first hint that something was wrong with Dad occurred in 1991. He and Mom were expected for a family dinner at our house. At that time we lived in our present home on Efland Drive in Northeast Greensboro. Usually punctual they were over an hour late that afternoon. Then my husband saw my father's white truck zoom right by our house. He and my son Joe ran to the car and followed them. Finally, my father pulled into a shopping strip to figure out why he couldn't get to our house, and my husband and son rescued them.

It was a sad day. My father's dementia, the secret Mom had struggled to hide, was now chillingly apparent. Later that week, I took my father to his family physician. After he referred Dad to a neurologist, my father was diagnosed with Alzheimer's. Uncomfortable as it made me feel, we were forced into using deception. We hid Dad's car keys. Later we hid his guns.

Gradually my father became more and more argumentative, and at night he would often wake up, stumble to the kitchen, and leave a faucet running. Hallucinations were the most frightening aspect of his illness. Once he claimed he witnessed the next door neighbor, a frail octogenarian, dig up the large redbud trees planted along the edge of her yard, then replant them on his property. He believed that she was attempting to fudge the property line in her favor. If my heart hadn't ached so much, I would have laughed. Another time, before we hid his guns, he took his shotgun into the back yard attempting to blast invisible trespassers.

My mother had congestive heart failure, yet despite her illness, she insisted on continuing to take care of my father and brother. Because she had never learned to drive, and my father and brother could no longer do so, my help was needed to pick up their groceries and prescriptions and to take them to numerous doctor appointments.

Dutifully, though not always enthusiastically, I drove down 220 South two or three times a week, doing whatever had to be done.

I felt particularly sorry for my mother during those difficult years. She'd always sacrificed so much for family. How I wished I'd spent more time with her. Determined to make up for the neglect, on days when I had time to do so, I took her on jaunts to Greensboro. She loved to tour old houses. Once we went to Blandwood to see how Governor John Motley Morehead and his family had lived. My mother had her own memories of the historic home. During the first half of the twentieth century, Blandwood was owned by the Keeley Institute, a place for recovering alcoholics. My mother knew two successful businessmen in Randleman who went there from time to time for *the cure*. The cure included gold shots, and clients were provided a homey atmosphere in exchange for sobriety. Sometimes, when my mother and father happened to be in Greensboro during the 1940s and 1950s, they glimpsed the historic home. Mother remembered men playing croquet on the lawn.

Visiting Blandwood brought bittersweet memories. The parents of my poet friend, Margaret Boothe Baddour, had managed the Keeley Institute. Unfortunately, while Margaret was still quite young, her parents were killed in an airplane crash. Margaret, who now lives in Goldsboro, is writing a book based on the childhood years she spent in that historic home. The portions I've read are poignant and compelling.

Another home Mom and I planned to see in Greensboro was the boarding house that had been owned by my mother's Aunt Lucy. Unfortunately, Mom couldn't recall the directions for getting there, so we never located it. Finally, deciding it had probably been demolished for road construction, we gave up the search.

But as I drove my mother home that day, I listened attentively as she described some of boarders who'd once lived there. A story that made her laugh every time she told it involved a gentleman by the name of Pless. In the boarding house, whenever green peas were included in the dinner menu, one boarder would say loudly, "Pless, pass the peas please." Mom found the alliteration hilarious and could never tell the story all the way through without collapsing in giggles. .

My mother had been in High Point with her mother and father, Flossie and Thomas Jetter Butler, when a tornado touched down in Greensboro on April 2, 1936. She sometimes spoke of how concerned they had been about Aunt Lucy and her boarding house that day. Though the boarding house was not in the direct line of the storm, the house was damaged but, fortunately, Aunt Lucy and her boarders were not hurt. The fierce twister destroyed many buildings and killed more than a dozen people. Any time I speak to someone who witnessed the aftermath, they relate vivid descriptions of the terror and destruction.

Aunt Lucy had three children, all brought up in Greensboro. Her daughter Euneta graduated from Greensboro College. Later, she moved to Georgia where she became a school principal. One of Aunt Lucy's sons, Charles, was a successful realtor, who once ran for the U.S. Senate, and the other son, George, was a businessman.

Both Aunt Lucy and her father (my great-grandfather), are now buried side by side in Forest Lawn Cemetery. Sometimes when I walk in Country Park or trek along picturesque

Battleground trails, I take a detour and visit them.

My mother was so easy to please that simply viewing the outside of older homes satisfied her. Sometimes I'd drive her through some of Greensboro's older neighborhoods, such as Fisher Park, Irving Park, Sedgefield, Starmount Forest, or Hamilton Lakes. Later, we'd go out to eat. She usually opted for the K&W Cafeteria located in Friendly Shopping Center. She said she preferred having the opportunity to see what she'd be eating before it showed up on her plate.

My mother loved pretty clothes and because she was slender, any outfit looked perfect on her. Sometimes I took her to shop at Friendly Shopping Center. Once at Belk's Department Store, after I'd advised her on outfits, she said, "Sandra, you're so good at helping people select clothes. You should work in a department store."

That remark irritated me, for she'd never praised my teaching or writing, but one Saturday afternoon a few weeks later, she made up for it. That afternoon, I took her to the Cultural Arts Center, located on Davie Street in downtown Greensboro. The building, originally owned by the *Greensboro Daily News* (now the *News & Record*), became a center for the arts after the newspaper moved into the larger building constructed on East Market Street. The former headquarters for the paper, now known as the Cultural Arts Center, contains artistic works by various ethnic groups. Classes, including dance, pottery, visual arts, and acting are also sponsored by the Center and VisionQuest, a special place for youngster, allows children to explore their creativity in several art media.

That particular afternoon I'd brought my mother to see *Pitstop*, a play produced by Brenda Schleunes and performed by the Touring Theatre of North Carolina. One of my short stories, "Tin of Tuberose," was incorporated into the play. My mother's face turned red with anger when a man in the audience announced that he didn't approve of the startling dialogue used in my story.

"Then you must not believe in freedom of speech," Mom told the astonished gentleman.

In 1995 both my parents were diagnosed with colon cancer. My father underwent surgery in March, and Mother's operation took place three months later. Both surgeries were performed at Moses Cone Hospital. Confused, my father needed a family member always by his side while in the hospital, but the surgery proved successful. My mother wasn't as lucky. Because of her weak heart, she developed complications and needed to be watched closely.

One evening, as I sat by her bed, an alarm rang out. Mom, though sick and hooked up to an IV, hopped out of bed and rushed for the door, dragging the IV with her. Fortunately, a nurse showed up immediately, informing us that the alarm had been set off by someone smoking in an elevator. Seeing how quickly Mom responded gave me hope that she would be okay. Three days later, grateful to Moses Cone Hospital and her fine doctors, she was finally allowed to return home.

The next few months, I worked at recovering from the stress and anxiety I suffered due to the illnesses of my family members. I realized that to give them the care they deserved, I needed to be full of vim and vitamins, so I did my best to follow the tongue-in-cheek health advice of Mark Twain: "Eat what you don't want, drink what you don't like and do what you'd rather not." I also paused for deep breaths whenever I had a few moments and did my best to simply live in the moment, shunning regrets over the past and resisting fears concerning the future. I walked whenever I could, sometimes in Greensboro's beautiful Anniversary Park, sometimes at Guilford Battleground, guarded by the noble statue of General Nathaniel Greene who led his troops against the English in the most crucial battle of the Revolutionary War.

Those years were busy. I had signed a contract with Community Communications of Montgomery, Alabama to complete a book, *Greensboro: Portrait of Progress* in seven months. Although I had other local writers working on some of the chapters and an excellent photographer, Mark Wagoner, and Illustrator, Bill Mangum, there was a great deal of research, writing, and organization needed to bring the project to completion. At that time, I was also teaching three classes at Guilford Technical Community College.

Though I really didn't have the time to spare, when my brother Mick asked if I would take him to Cherokee, North Carolina to research our genealogy, I agreed to do so. We both needed to get away from the constant reminders of our parents' declining health. During those three days, we felt renewed by the impressive mountain vistas, even though we failed in Mick's purpose: He'd hoped to find the names of enough of our ancestors on the tribal rolls to substantiate that we were at least 1/16th Cherokee. If that fact could be established, we would be eligible for a miniscule percentage of the profits made by Harrah's Casino built on the Cherokee Reservation. From my father's appearance and all the family stories passed down by family, we felt certain that more than enough Cherokee blood flowed through our veins. Alas, my father's grandmother, a full-blooded Cherokee, never signed the Cherokee rolls. Many of the

Cherokees, particularly women who married white men, resisted having their names recorded there.

Curiously, I had the characteristic coloring and features of a Cherokee. My brother, the one intent on verifying our heritage, had red hair and freckles.

Once we returned home, I was touched when my brother told me, "You'll never know how much the trip meant to me." When younger, he'd traveled extensively in the United States and abroad. But the trip we made to Cherokee was the last place beyond Randolph and Guilford Counties that he ever traveled.

In 1997, I impulsively purchased a white Voltzwagen convertible. I'd never owned a convertible before, but had always envisioned myself cruising down the highway, letting the wind blow through my hair. That little car immediately spiced up my life. My grandsons loved riding in it, and so did my father. Sometimes, he would put on his Panthers ball cap and accompany me to pick up a prescription or a loaf of bread.

I wanted to take my mother to visit my son Michael who lived at Myrtle Beach, but I felt uneasy leaving Dad alone for three days. My brother assured me he'd be able to look after him. Together we contacted a short list of those we could depend on in an emergency. Finally, comfortable that my brother and father would be okay, Mom and I whizzed off in the convertible, both of us wearing stylish sunglasses. Before we traveled as far as Asheboro, she pulled a pink scarf from her purse to protect her hair.

My son was elated to see Mom but concerned over how fragile she'd become. Despite her declining health, Mom drank a glass of wine with Mike and me. She looked forward, she said, to seeing the ocean once again. The next day we took her to the beach, down near the edge of the water, where she sat in a lounge chair, protected from wind by a yellow beach towel.

1998 was a topsy-turvy year, filled with many peaks and valleys. Though I made frequent trips to Randleman, I still managed to continue working by writing and teaching.
Greensboro: A Portrait of Progress, the book I'd spent so much time completing, came out. I also published articles and reviews in several regional magazines, including *Elegant Bride* and *Our State.* And I continued to write book reviews for the *News & Record.* Additionally I taught both curriculum and continuing education writing courses.

My husband and I had been comfortably coasting financially, until Rolane, where he was employed, went belly up. He had always worked, so after nearly a year of helping close the stores, located throughout the United States, I urged him to take some time off for himself. For years he'd wanted to hike the Appalachian Trail. After retiring from Rolane, he did trek many of the sections in North Carolina and Virginia, but soon, reverting back to his previous workaholic ways, he went searching for another job.

Though he spent a few years locating a position that suited him, he eventually accepted a position working for John Lonergan at Croscill outlet stores. John, congenial and kind hearted, had once worked for Joe at Rolane.

Though Joe had little formal computer training, his position was to manage the computer system used by the outlets. He had already taken to computers as effortlessly as a frog takes to a pond. Now, still working part-time for Croscill, he not only answers all the employees' questions about computers, he also helps out friends who get tangled up in the latest technology. Additionally, he currently maintains three websites in addition to his own.

For his next birthday, I just might purchase a gold cape imprinted with a big white C for my COMPUTERMAN. He certainly deserves recognition for his knowledge and dedication.

A Measured Beat

The rhythm of my days changed as my family required more and more attention. At first, I'd tried to tend to my parents and do everything else as well. Soon I realized that wasn't possible. I would have to relinquish teaching temporarily.

I was "ghost writing" a book at that time. I was also finishing up a book about Winston-Salem for Community Communications. One problem: I wouldn't be paid for either until completed. In the meantime I wanted to earn money, so I made a phone call to Measurement, a company that paid employees every two weeks.

Measurement, Inc. is located in the Spring Valley Shopping Center on the South side of Greensboro. According to their web page, this company is "an employee-owned corporation that contracts with state and local departments of education, other educational agencies, and private businesses to develop and score educational tests." The Greensboro office of Measurement is one of twelve scattered throughout the United States. The building, long and unimpressive on the outside, houses a bevy of activity on the inside.

Though there are only a few full-time positions at Measurement, the company locally hires hundreds of temporary workers. For over fifteen years I'd worked from time to time for Measurement. I genuinely enjoyed the job, which involved a great deal of reading. Another perk: the company provided free coffee. But those reasons are just the cream inside the doughnut. The main reason I always loved going through those doors was the great diversity of people I encountered.

This company is, in essence, a microcosm of Greensboro. Measurement makes sure that people of all races, ethic groups, and religions have an equal opportunity to work and advance there. Whenever I signed onto a project, I met intelligent men and women I could learn from. Many of them became friends.

During one project, my team leader was a young man who'd traveled to every corner of the globe. While working there last year, I interviewed and wrote an article about John Nagbe, a grandfather who'd come to Greensboro from his native country, Liberia, to escape bloody massacres. Another employed senior citizen, Dr. Tom Moore, in his eighties, is a retired Professor of Business at Guilford College. "Dr. Tom," brings a keen sense of humor with him every time he walks through Measurement's doors. And Maggie Fonge, an entrepreneur extraordinare, came with her husband from Cameroon in African, seeking better educational and business opportunities for herself, her husband, and their five children.

While earning my M.F.A. in Creative Writing at the University of North Carolina in Greensboro, I accepted my first assignment at Measurement. I preferred the night shift since I had classes during the day. Sharin Francis, a writer I'd known from years before, worked there. During dinner break, we caught up, recalling the time we'd been in the same writing group. I'd always admired Sharin, but once again I was reminded of her intelligence and determination. As a single parent of two lovely daughters, she managed to rear them and earn a B.A. in English. Now she delights in mentoring her granddaughters. Sharin, a loyal friend, is proof that hard work pays off. Like me, her interests are broad and varied. Recently, the two of us attended a drum circle at Ten Thousand Villages. Now Sharin wants to play an African drum, and I've decided to purchase a Native American tom-tom.

There were other aspiring writers working at night and a few artists, among them Janet Schafer, whose colorful free-spirited paintings I absolutely love. One of her larger works brightens my living room. Because Janet frequently uses her own blue fingerprints in her paintings, she's adopted Dottie Blue as her artist name.

Many employees working at night taught school during the day. I always admired them. I wondered if, like me, they found peace in the concentration required for reading papers written by students. Focusing on the work became a great blessing. For brief periods of time, it freed my mind of troubling thoughts of family illnesses.

When I took assignments during the day, the manager was Bobbie Henderson, an intelligent sweet woman, dedicated to keeping the work site clean and pleasant for all. The receptionist, Betty Rose, a spirited blonde kept up with articles and stories I'd written, and touted my accomplishments to others. We both shared a love of reading. I highly valued her opinions of both my own writing and the writing of others.

In my attempt to describe Measurement, I'm reminded of Walt Whitman's celebratory poem, *I Hear America Singing*. In it, he catalogues all the various types that make up this country. I only wish I had Whitman's poetic flair to describe the wonderful souls I worked with while there.

Evelyn Edwards always remained at the top of my list of favorite co-workers. Petite and vivacious, with her gray hair always styled and her fingernails painted pink, she once told me that she had worked for Measurement since the company located in Greensboro. Before then she'd taught school for over thirty years and later worked at a nursing home so she could be near her blind sister. Her employment at Measurement lasted until she reached her ninetieth birthday.

Evelyn, possessing seniority, looked after the rest of us. When someone new walked through the door, she introduced herself, then proudly announced her age. For special occasions, she brought peanut brittle. Once, she confessed to me that she never ate hard candy, but liked to make others happy by bringing it to Measurement. If anyone failed to include a fork or spoon with the lunch brought from home, she always had an extra one to share. But the most appreciated favor of all was Evelyn's dinner bell. When it was time for break, Evelyn boldly rang the tiny silver bell, ignoring that we hadn't been dismissed by management. When Evelyn placed the bell on the table once more, we rose together, all of us heading toward the door.

Even at ninety, Evelyn still enjoyed a good time. Once I asked her why she was laughing. She replied "because it feels so good." Everyone has an Achilles heel. Evelyn's was gambling. Sometimes a game of Bingo would suffice, but the big thrill for her was flying to Atlantic City to play the slots. Whenever she planned to head out on one of her gambling adventures, she wore her special ball cap, covered with pins from the casinos where she'd played. Her request on those days was for everyone to touch her hat for luck.

Evelyn died a few weeks after her ninety-fourth birthday. I still have fond memories of attending one of the three birthday parties given for her that last year. She laughed as she opened gifts and ate birthday cake. She kissed everyone on the cheek. That was Evelyn: Measurement's party girl.

Marilyn Carter, who also worked at Measurement, became Evelyn's dear friend. Before Evelyn died, she visited her at least once a week, bringing mints or other gifts. I once asked Marilyn, who had many other obligations, the reason for her devotion to the friend she'd worked with at Measurement. She replied that she enjoyed Evelyn's company. To her, she seemed almost like a mother.

In recent years, when I've worked at Measurement, I walk during the first part of my lunch break. Often Karen Leonard, a quiet young woman devoted to her church and her children, walks with me. In recent years both of Karen's parents died, still she continues to smile, believing tomorrow will be better despite obstacles that temporarily block the way. Another walking buddy, Terry Thomas, has also had more than her share of hard knocks. Still, she remains spunky as she cares for her mother who has cancer.

Another frequent walker, Jo Jane Pitt, graduated, like me, from the M.F.A. writing program at the University of North Carolina in Greensboro. Though Jo Jane doesn't write now, she earns money by editing the writing of others. Susan Getty, an avid hiker, makes tracks faster than any of us, getting back to

Measurement's building in time to read articles from *The New Yorker* while eating her lunch.

One table I gravitate to during lunch seats several women. They debate, they laugh, and they form a small community of cohesiveness despite their varied backgrounds. Each has their own area of expertise: Frankie Luther loves cinema. Before going to a movie theatre, I always ask her for recommendations. As yet, she's never steered me wrong. Julie Campbell, who is writing a fantasy novel, shares with me the agony and ecstasy of being a writer, and Jean Haddock, who knows everyone at Measurement, provides a beaming smile while mentioning all the outstanding accomplishments of her fellow workers. Tangela Stanley, a gifted singer, loves stories and music. Tangela's life *is* a song; mine is a dance. Once I invited Tangela to a reading I did at the public library. She emailed me that she'd be out of town that day, but that her husband and son would come instead. That's real friendship.

Every time I begin another project at Measurement, I feel as if I have a roomful of willing partners to share any of the hops, skips, and sways that might come my way. Measurement is a perfect place to "Make new friends, but keep the old. One is silver; the other is gold."

Danse Macabre

In February, 1998, when Mom had her yearly physical, Dr. Vyas recommended a colonoscopy. Quiet and sincere, he had helped both my mother and father fight several illnesses. Still; I wondered why he wanted her to have a colonoscopy, since she'd had a portion of her colon removed less than a year before. Still, following his instructions, we scheduled an appointment for the procedure.

The day before the colonoscopy, I went to stay with Mom so I could assist her with the prescribed cleansing. She had to drink a gallon jug of a vile tasting liquid to prepare her body for the procedure. This was unpleasant for both of us. The liquid kept making Mom nauseous; she never finished all of it.

Because her appointment was early the next morning, I spent the night at her house. Exhausted by caring for her and attempting to keep my father, who thought I was torturing Mom, at bay, I expected to immediately go to sleep once my head touched the pillow. But sleep is often difficult for me, particularly when I'm stressed. A rude host that evening, sleep denied me the pleasure of his company, so I tossed and turned, troubling thoughts uncoiling in my restless mind. Finally, just before dawn, I sank into a deep sleep that took me to another realm, one that failed to provide the peace I desperately desired. I dreamed that I'd paused while taking a long hike. As I stood on a wooded pier overlooking a murky bog, I noticed something move. Whatever it was, it was huge, still I felt protected and safe, for the creature was in a swamp. Suddenly an enormous anaconda leapt out of the water. In my inconsistent nightmare, when the big snake wrapped around my leg, I was no longer near the bog. Instead I was in bed, trapped, unable to move.

The dream sank unrelentingly into my consciousness that day. I've always been guided by dreams. This nightmare vision, I believed, was a warning. Later, after Mom's colonoscopy, she was referred to a surgeon. The anaconda of my dream, just as I'd feared, signaled the return of cancer.

In April of 1998, an MRI confirmed my suspicion. That wasn't even the bad news. The MRI revealed that the cancer had spread from the colon to the liver. Later, when I was shown the X-ray, I was stunned by the shape of the blob, which resembled a snake.

The surgeon referred us to Dr. Karb, a Greensboro Oncologist.

Dr. Karb had a wonderful sense of humor as well as a deep respect for patients. He spoke succinctly and honestly, informing Mom that since the cancer was large and positioned in the center of the liver, it was inoperable. Treatments were available that would slow the progress, but liver cancer did not usually respond well to chemo. Because she was in her eighties and had congestive heart failure, Mom decided not to aggressively seek a solution.

My brother and I started asking questions and reading everything we could find. All the news was bad. Mom, I'm sure, must have already suspected before the MRI. Though concerned about my father and brother, she faced the possibility of death with stoicism. Life has many seasons, I recall her saying, and winter eventually comes to everyone. I felt certain that she put on a brave face to avoid upsetting my brother and me. Because she'd rationalized three of her brothers' deaths by saying they'd lived their "three score and ten" (70), she decided that at 82, she'd made it past four score, a perfectly reasonable time to spend on this earth.

I've always admired her courage. She took care of her mother who lived to be 90 and then her brother Ralph who died at 70. Additionally, for several years she cared for my father and brother as their health deteriorated.

I vowed to do my best to follow her saintly example, calmly taking one day at a time. But I was not my mother. I desperately wanted miracle cures for her, for my father, and for my brother. I demanded more information from Dr. Karb. How long? I asked. "Maybe as much as six months," he said. I offered to move in with Mom and Dad, but both Mom and my brother decided that for the time being they could manage with my coming down several times a week. At that point, Mom still had few cancer symptoms, except for fatigue.

Her surgeon convinced her to have the colon surgery. Otherwise she would soon be in agony. Though I worried that she might not survive the operation, she actually fared better than she had after her first operation. Still she needed a great deal of care. I had been going down two to three times a week to Randleman, now I'd need to go more often.

In contrast to the cloud that hung over my parents, the sun couldn't have been brighter for my two sons. Both had fallen in love and before the year ended, both would marry.

The eldest had been married before. His two sons, Ben and Dave, were bright lights in my life. But now my son Joey had found someone else. Her name was Janet Johnston. An attractive dark-haired woman, she adored being outside. At the time she lived in an isolated historic home in Snow Camp, a small community located in Alamance County. Fond of animals, she had many pets, including cats, dogs, ducks, a hare and a squirrel. Large noble trees grew on the property along with abundant beds of calla lilies she'd planted.

Her lifestyle meshed with my son's, for he, too, had always loved being outside. Another shared interest was preparing food. Previously, both had attended Alamance Community College where they worked on culinary degrees. My son, who had previously owned a pizza parlor, presently worked for food services at the Chapel Hill Hospital. Janet, who'd once been a waitress, managed a school cafeteria.

Mom, deciding she was well enough to attend, asked if I'd take her shopping for something to wear. After one of her many doctor appointments, we stopped by Penny's at Four Season's Mall. For the wedding she settled on a pink linen skirt, a cream-colored silk blouse, and a striking jacket printed with pastel spring flowers. It suited her, but the jacket looked too big. "Mom," I advised, "You need a smaller size."

She objected. "This one feels fine, but I want you to try it on."

"Why?"

"I'll know if it's the right choice when I see it on someone else."

When I reluctantly put the coat on, she smiled. Later she confessed that she knew that she wouldn't be getting much wear out of it. She intended that I have it after she was gone.

Mom, though a bit unsteady, did attend my son's wedding. Because we never knew what Dad might do, he was left at home with Mick who had in recent months become more and more reclusive.

That May day in 1998 was lovely. My daughter-in-law looked radiant in her wedding dress. Her lovely teenage daughter Alice, served as Maid of Honor. The reception, held at a community center in Alamance County, was filled with good will. I recall hugging everyone—my grandsons, my son, his wife and her mother. Sharing the happy occasion felt good, and I was especially grateful that my mother could be there.

The following week, I received a frantic phone call from my brother. Mother was itching; nothing seemed to help. I'd planned to go to Randleman the next day. Mick said he thought it could wait. In the meantime, they would try Gold Bond powder.

When I arrived the next morning, Mom had red scratch marks all over her hands and arms. She couldn't keep from clawing the spots that itched. "It's worse than poison ivy," she told me. When I called Dr. Karb and described the itching, he asked that we bring her in the next day. In the meantime, he would call in a prescription to control the itching. He also suggested that I buy white cotton gloves for Mom to wear. I frantically drove everywhere searching for white cotton gloves. Finally, in a costume shop, I located a pair. At the time, desperately yearning for just one ray of sunshine, finding the gloves seemed a major triumph.

The next morning the drive to Greensboro was grim. Though it was a hot day, Mom felt cool, so I turned off the air conditioning. A sickening stench of fear filled my convertible. Was it my mother's fear or my own? Then, unexpectedly, Mom told me she wasn't afraid. "I'm just miserable from the itching," she said. The sun made everything so bright and clear, it hurt my eyes. I glanced at Mom, and then looked away hoping she hadn't seen the shocked expression on my face. Her skin had a slight yellow cast to it. *Jaundice.* The dreaded word floated through my mind. When the liver isn't functioning properly, the skin and even the whites of a person's eyes, turn yellow. I'd read about it while searching through articles to learn more about her cancer.

As we drove down Elm Street on the way to Dr. Karb's office, I became very talkative, attempting to camouflage the fear that gripped me.

There's the First Presbyterian Church, I told my mother, once the largest church in all of Greensboro. Next, we passed Fisher Park, not very large but, nevertheless, a tranquil park. Sometimes I walk all the way from my house to here, I told Mom.

She glanced out the window. "Nice houses," she said.

"Yes," I agreed. "This is where Greensboro's founders intended the center city to be, but because much of this area was then a duck pond, they decided against it."

Mom laughed, as she continued to rub her itching arms. The cotton gloves had helped. Her arms were no longer bleeding.

Avoiding talk of her illness, I pointed out a tall building on the left. "That's the Hampshire," I told her. "When that building first opened during the 1960's, it was called the Towers. The most expensive apartments in all of Greensboro were there. I remember people wondering why those living in the Towers didn't buy houses instead."

I turned right at the next road. Cone Hospital, a sprawling yellow building stretched out on the left. A block beyond it, I turned to the right, then into the large medical building that housed Dr. Karb's office.

As usual Dr. Karb began by joking. This time it was a comment about his large nose. That day I couldn't manage a laugh, but Mom smiled bravely. Dr. Karb confirmed my suspicion: Mom was jaundiced.

Without shedding a tear, she asked Dr. Karb, "How long?"

I can't remember his answer. The time frame was probably so short that I blocked it out. I do know that she lived longer than any of us expected. Apparently, if you're older, your metabolism slows, which also slows the growth of cancer. However long mother had, she needed help. Dr. Karb suggested Hospice. It was time now for me to move in with her.

Later, when I talked to my husband Joe, he agreed. My Mom, Dad, and brother needed me, and he, too, would do whatever he could to help.

With Mom's consent, we contacted Hospice of Randolph County. They would assist with Mom's physical care, they informed us, and answer any of her questions about legal and medical issues. They'd also be there for Mick and me, when we needed a shoulder to cry on.

I was needed almost every hour of every day. I slept on a cot in the living room. My brother, fighting his own disability, slept late in the mornings in his garage apartment, then joined us for lunch. After the meal, as long as Mom remained able to do so, we'd take her to the flower garden, enclosed beside the house in a stone wall. It was her favorite retreat. Within an hour, she'd be exhausted, needing to nap or rest for a while.

Mick also needed a great deal of rest, but he would return to the house to sit with Mom long enough for me to take my afternoon walk. Usually, to clear my head, I'd walk down High Point Street until I came to the bridge over Deep River. Sometimes, during those brief respites, I wondered how the dam would change Greensboro and Randleman, but most of the time I thought only of my mother or my husband. Though I knew he was fine by himself, I missed Joe a great deal during the weeks I lived in Randleman. I particularly missed the walks we enjoyed in Greensboro.

Located on Hobbs Road, the Bog Garden, has long been one of our favorite spots. Serene in winter, the bog becomes a quacking menagerie, filled with new born ducks in spring, and by summer, harmless water snakes clog the waterfall. And the city's watershed trails remain always lovely, even when lakes become pockmarked by drought. I once counted fourteen herons while walking the Peninsula Trail. The Townsend Trail, kept pristine by the Sierra Club, stands tall with towering birches, their reflections in the lake making them twins. Battleground, designated a national park, is a trail of history. Above ground are hero statues; below lie the hallowed bodies of soldiers who lost their lives during the American Revolution. Frisky squirrels and leaping deer claim the park for their own during early mornings, then shy away as two-legged visitors invade their paradise.

Of all the parks, Bur-Mil, located off Lawndale Drive, is the one Joe and I hike most. This great gift, bestowed to the city by

Burlington Mills, invites runners, cyclers, and hikers to vie for space on trails sweetly scented with pine needles. There's also Laurel Bluff and Reedy Fork, the two comely trails enclosing Lake Brandt.

The trees on all those trails remain glorious, whether dressed in the brilliant hues of autumn or stripped naked by the wily winds of winter. The smell of dead leaves beneath our feet comforts us and the sound of water rushing over rocks whisper of eternity.

Yes, I missed my husband and Greensboro, during those days when sadness surrounded my family, thick as fog. But during the brief hour I walked each afternoon while in Randleman, bright glimmers of sun promised happier days ahead.

Some days I was tempted to throw my hands up and forget the family dance I'd accepted. One morning, Mom's blood pressure dropped so low she turned blue. Another time, medication prescribed for her, to help control the dreadful itching, caused her to hallucinate. She believed goblins were in the room. A few weeks later, she began trembling. And finally, it became almost impossible for her to eat or talk.

During those sad months, I appreciated the encouraging notes and phone calls from friends in Greensboro. When Anne Barnhill telephoned, saying she planned to drive to Randleman to see me, I was elated.

That day I arranged to be away long enough to have lunch with Anne. After she visited briefly with Mom, we both hopped into my convertible and, gleeful as two school girls, headed out. The sun shone brightly on us as we drove to a restaurant in nearby Asheboro. Anything would have tasted great that day. For a few minutes I could relax as Anne updated me with all the good, bad, and ugly going on in her own life. Even more important, I could unload all my own grief and concerns. Anne is always a sympathetic listener.

As my friend and I sat in the restaurant, topping off our lunch with slices of cheesecake, I glanced out the window. Rain pounded down on my convertible. Oh, no, I told Anne. I'd left the top down. By the time we reached the car, the inside was soaked. Oh, well, I decided, and then, raising my arms in defeat, I began laughing and dancing in the rain.

My worst times, during that long, hot summer, resulted not from my Mom's illness but rather from my father's. He didn't understand why mother couldn't get out of bed. He had to be watched or he'd head for her bedroom and try pulling her up. We'd explain, but he'd forget. Because he frequently got up during the night, I had difficulty sleeping. My brother and I decided that it was definitely time to find a safe place for our father, a place where he wouldn't hurt himself or anyone else. We both dreaded discussing it with Mom, but when we finally talked to her, she agreed that finding an Alzheimer's facility for him was necessary.

I visited several facilities in Asheboro. My brother, by computer and telephone, researched the three that I considered best suited for Dad. We quickly settled on Crossroad, a Baptist-sponsored retirement home with an Alzheimer's unit.

After staff members came to Mom and Dad's house and interviewed each of us, Cross Road agreed to accept Dad, but because the facility was so popular, we were advised to take him there as soon as a room became available. The day before my birthday, we received a call letting us know that a room was available. Though I dreaded taking Dad to the facility, I helped him dress the next morning, suggesting that he wear his favorite ball cap. I explained that I was taking him to a place that might be able to help him with his memory. Of course, he thought it would be like a doctor's appointment and he'd return home in an hour or so. I'd packed his suitcase earlier and hid it in the trunk of my car.

Once there, one of the attendants convinced Dad to go with him. I filled out the necessary paper work, then, with a heavy heart, took Dad's suitcase to the room assigned to him. I'd been instructed to leave as soon as I'd unpacked his things. Though that had been my intention, just as I left the room, my father, a tall man weighing nearly 200 pounds, came bounding toward me, the frantic attendant attempting to catch up with him. "Oh Lordy, Sandra, I didn't think I'd ever find you," my father shouted out.

Though my heart fell into pieces, I looked my father in the eye and lied: "You need to stay a while longer. I'll be back soon." Then kissing him on the cheek, I left him there, the attendant holding his arms.

Because it was my birthday, I'd planned to go home long enough to enjoy dinner and a video with my husband. I've rarely felt more miserable than I did that afternoon. It's all just too much, I recall thinking, as I drove toward Greensboro. Tears filled my eyes. Unable to drive, I pulled off the road long enough to have a good cry.

Once at my home in Greensboro, I looked around the yard. The beautiful azaleas that my husband had planted years before were in bloom. Joe had cleaned the house. While I relaxed with a glass of wine, he cooked steaks on the grill. Then we watched a video, *Message in a Bottle* on Television. That evening the message in my mind was that yes, I could do whatever still needed to be done for my parents and my brother. I smiled at my husband, knowing that I didn't have to do it alone. Hospice would be there helping me, and so would he.

Less than a month later, the hospice nurse informed me that mother probably wouldn't last through the day, After I called family members, all of us gathered around her, except for my son Michael who lived in Myrtle Beach. He couldn't leave until the next morning, but that evening he telephoned. Though Mom hadn't been able to talk for almost a week, she managed to say she loved him. When we put her to bed, everyone left except Mick and me. My brother stayed with Mom for a couple hours so I could get some rest. Then I relieved him before midnight, sitting in a chair beside Mom. Soon the fish out of water breathing, a gasping sound that proceeds death, began. The next morning, I left Mom's bedside long enough to take the trash outside. The sun was bright; the wind, calm.

My mother left us later that morning. My brother Mick held one of her hands; I held the other. After a final breath, her face relaxed and she looked peaceful. As soon as I called Hospice, they were there, our angels on earth, holding us up as we walked through the shadows.

LEARNING TO DANCE AGAIN

After my mother died, I felt leaden, as if within my chest something heavy weighed me down. But there was little time to properly grieve, for I still needed to care for my brother and father and put my Mom's house in order. Additionally, I needed to finish the Winston-Salem book, so setting aside time for research was mandatory.

What consoled me most was that I could move from Randleman back into my own house, thus spending more time with my husband. During those sad days, my children and friends were very sweet, comforting me with cards, flowers, or simply by being there, listening as, over glasses of wine or iced tea, I released bit by bit the bitter grief that burdened me.

Isn't it strange how the sad and happy moments in life meld together? Mom died in May and in June of that year our son Mike married Tina Williamson, a lovely young woman who could throw a soft ball as fast as any woman in South Carolina. She and Michael had so much in common. They both loved living at the coast and they both loved sports and dogs. My husband and

I were excited for them, and though I hadn't had time to make preparations before Mom died, we quickly selected a place for the rehearsal dinner and explored what we might do to make the occasion special for them. I wrote a poem about them and their dog Moogie: I ended it with the following lines: Some day, Moog will have a sister/If not a sister, a brother will do. My son maintained that he and Tina didn't plan to have children. It wasn't on their agenda. I never believed them, not for one minute.

The June wedding, held at Licthfield Country Club on Pawley's Island, was lovely. Not even the rain storm, making the planned "outdoor wedding" impossible, dampened spirits. My husband served as best man just as he had for our eldest son and Joey was one of the ushers. Tina's sister, Beth, served as honor attendant. The reception, planned by Tina's parents, Butch and Carol Anne Williamson, was a joyous celebration of music, dancing, and champagne. I remember dancing the night away. For a while all sadness was forgotten.

After returning from the wedding, I began devoting my time, once again, to the care of my father and brother. Eventually realizing that I couldn't continue to help others without making time for myself, I mapped out a new plan: I'd be available whenever my father and brother needed me for five days a week. But, except for emergencies, I'd keep the weekends free. During those leisurely Saturdays and Sundays, I became reacquainted with Greensboro.

Each Saturday morning, the *News & Record* would be on the sidewalk in front of our house by 6:00 AM. After scanning headlines, I'd turn to the obituaries. My husband always joked, "Making sure you're not there, huh?" Then handing him the large crossword puzzle, I'd begin the smaller one while drinking a mug of the aromatic French Roast coffee he'd brewed even before I'd gotten out of bed. Once I'd figured out the puzzle, I'd give myself a check mark and turn to the classifieds searching for yard sales. Then, as now, I was afflicted with a springtime passion: rummaging through other people's cast offs, hoping to find treasures.

To be successful at yardsaling, it's important to set out early. Spring transforms Greensboro into one of the loveliest cities on the planet. So many different varieties of trees and flowers bloom, and the mornings are cooled by the moisture of dew. As I'd drive to one promising destination and then another, I often recalled Andrew Marvell"s poetic advice: "Gather ye rosebuds while ye may." Though his poem wasn't written specifically about procuring yard sale bargains, metaphorically it worked for me.

What incredible possessions people toss out. I've purchased valuable gold and silver jewelry sold off a dingy sheet covering the grass in someone's yard. A poignant original drawing of a Native American, purchased for two dollars, occupies a prominent place on my living room wall. Another phenomenal find was a face jug made by a Seagrove potter and a vase formed by Master Potter Ben Owen of Seagrove. I've also discovered a few rare books and even a large collection of arrowheads, clumped together in a dusty cardboard box. When I asked the owner if he was sure he didn't want to keep them, he replied, "I ain't got no use for em."

Going to the Farmers' Curb Market located on Yanceyville Street was another Saturday morning treat. The market, a delight to the senses, always has someone selling ham biscuits and hot coffee. By June, the produce tables overflow with cucumbers, corn, radishes, and peaches, fragrant and ready for purchase.

On Saturday evenings my husband would sometimes take me to a play or movie. Frequently we'd eat out with friends. Sunday's were reserved for walking some of Greensboro's trails or occasionally going out of town to the mountains, seeking a more strenuous hike. Whatever we did was a welcome respite. "No place like home," I recall thinking again and again.

In addition to writing, I accepted a part-time teaching position at Randolph Community College after my mother died. For a while I taught composition courses on Mondays and Wednesdays. Cross Road was less than three miles away, so I visited Dad between my morning and evening classes.

David Swartz, who managed the Alzheimer's unit at Cross Road, was always forthright with us. During the years my father resided there, David became both a friend to us and a friend to our father. A former minister, David actually lived the Biblical verse, "In as much as ye do it unto one of the least of these, ye have done it unto me." Though in charge, he selected the lowliest tasks for himself: Feeding and cleaning up after the dogs and birds and looking after some of the most unpleasant duties regarding the personal care of residents. Additionally, he became close to every person there, regardless of how disagreeable they might be. Though sometimes paranoid, due to his illness, my father came to respect and believe David.

After my last class, I could pick up groceries and prescriptions for my brother Mick, dropping them by his house before I drove back to Greensboro. I'd always come another day, usually Friday, to take my brother wherever he needed to go and help him with house cleaning.

During that time, Mick and I also had the sad task of sorting through Mom's possessions, deciding what to give away and what to keep. It was an arduous process because Mom's attic was stuffed with old magazines, clothing, furniture and books. We also had to make decisions about the upkeep of the house.

Despite staying busy, a deep sadness descended over me from time to time. Everyone in my family had cherished Mom. I missed her presence, but I also worried that I might not be doing enough for my father and brother. What would she expect me to do? I asked myself often. I didn't feel as capable as she had been nor as nurturing. I particularly worried that my brother was not well enough to be living on his own. Several times I asked him to consider moving to Greensboro, but he always insisted he was fine in Randleman.

One morning as I drove out West Market Street in Greensboro, I spotted something moving high on the hill that sloped down from the large brick building that had once housed Pilot Life Insurance Company. I pulled my car onto the side of the road and looked again. A beautiful doe with a fawn following close behind leapt halfway down the hill, then stopped, looking directly at me. After a few seconds she turned, rushing back up the hill, the small deer leaping behind her. Heading into a grove of trees, they disappeared.

At that moment, a peaceful feeling settled over me. I smiled, knowing that everything would be all right.

For me, the appearance of the mother deer became a positive omen. Later I decided that the deer somehow represented my mother. And the fawn? I believe it was the child me leaving with her. The message became clear: With my mother's death, I had to relinquish being a child. Instead time and circumstance had forced me into the role of family matriarch. Bowing my head that day, I accepted the responsibility. I could never replace you, I told my mother, but I promise to do my best to make you proud.

SURVIVING THE PASO DOBLE

The Paso Doble is a fierce dance. The movements resemble those of a matador and bull, each struggling to win a fight that ends in death.

As the millennium approached, I continued my own fight to keep my brother and father alive, but the shadow of death lengthened as their health continued to fail.

Even when in Greensboro, I couldn't forget them. Scary phone calls became more frequent: Cross Roads calling to let me know that Daddy refused to eat, had an impaction, or had fallen. Should they wait until I came down? Should they call an ambulance? My brother also called often, letting me know the roof was leaking, he was trapped inside his apartment with snow packed up outside the door, or had fallen. Any time the phone rang at night, dread washed over me.

Usually when my family gathers for Christmas, all of us act like a bunch of kids. That year I did put silly favors and lottery tickets in the stockings and each of us pulled apart the colorful crackers, a British tradition that we'd made our own, before we ate dinner. We even placed the thin paper King hats, found inside the crackers, on our heads and read the nonsensical jokes. I always had something red for everyone (REDding, get it?). That year it was socks. Still it wasn't quite the same. Mom was no longer with us and neither Dad nor Mick was well enough to join us.

Adding to my pessimism were the rumors, fueled by media, that when we began a new century computers would fail. Airline fares for flights scheduled on New Year's Eve dropped dramatically. More frightened than most, I imagined a hundred things going wrong. To help ease the anxiety, I began going for a walk every day. I also temporarily stopped frequenting Krispy Kreme, located quite near me on Battleground Avenue, for doughnuts and coffee. That was quite a sacrifice.

I don't think I slept at all on New Year's Eve, 1999. Yet despite my foolish fears, all remained well in Greensboro on January 1, 2000. I'd been afraid to celebrate the night before, but my husband and I did celebrate New Year's Day by cooking an abundance of pinto beans and collard greens. We ate until we were sated, and then ate more, happily embracing the notion that consuming such simple fare would bring luck and prosperity.

The millennium brought two surprises to Greensboro. The retail sales soared in January and snow fell twice that month, covering the landscape with crystal white brilliance. I still recall the squeals of happy children, wild with excitement as they careened their sleds down the slopes of the golf course of the Greensboro Country Club, and I recall opening the front door one morning to the splendor of the beautiful pine tree, its limbs heavy with snow, that majestically ruled the landscape in our neighbor's yard across the street.

Snow in Greensboro, a rarity, was almost always welcomed. But there's long been an odd tradition here. Soon as folks hear the slightest whisper that there might be snow, they put on their overcoats and head for the Harris Teeter or Food Lion for loaves of bread. I've seen empty bread shelves when not a single flake fell from the sky, simply because one of the weather forecasters said, "There's some possibility of ..."

Greensboro rarely has bad weather. Except for a few tornados, one of them nearly a century ago, and one this year, in May, 2008, we have miraculously avoided major disasters. Still more than a few destructive storms have caused power failures and uprooted large trees. Greensboro's biggest weather threat might be the possibility of getting struck by lightning while on a golf course. Personally, I'm not aware of that happening, but I do know local residents who've been hit by golf balls. I also know people who collect them if they land on their property. Mary Beisner, a local writer with a buoyant personality, lives across the street from the Sedgefield Golf Course. In her house, she keeps a huge decorative tub filled with golf balls. When I commented on there being so many, she noted that those were just the marked ones found on her property. She gives the unmarked ones to a young boy who attends her church.

Though I'd worried myself literally sick over my brother and father's health and baseless millennium fears, the really frightening event happened nearly two years later on a calm morning, not a cloud in the sky. I credit myself with being intuitive, but I had no premonition of the misfortune that descended that day as I drove toward Randolph Community College to teach my morning class.

Classical music flowed from the public radio station. Then, after a sudden break in programming, a strange news bulletin delivered unease. A plane had crashed into the World Trade Center in New York City, the announcer said. Then the public broadcasting system returned to a composition by Beethoven.

Well, that's weird, I thought. The date was September 11, 2001, a day that would become even weirder as the day unfolded.

By the time I reached the community college, another plane had crashed into the trade center. Still, no one seemed to realize the implication. My hands felt cold as ice cubes. My mind raced. What the hell did it mean? I wondered. As soon as I reached the community college, I telephoned my brother, waking him up. When I told him what had happened, he said, "Not again," referring to the bombing incident at the Trade Center a few years before. Soon as I dismiss my class, I'll come to Randleman, I told him.

Oddly, most of my students had not heard the news. I taught the class, staying as calm as possible. By the time I'd finished, a plane had crashed into the Pentagon. After dismissing my class, I drove to Randleman where Mick and I both listened to the news bulletins on television. I called the community college. They still planned to have classes that evening. I called Cross Road. They said that my father was oblivious to what had happened. "We'll take good care of him," the attendant assured me. I telephoned my husband. Though I felt as if the world might be ending, his voice remained calm, reassuring. "I have to teach tonight," I said. "Get in touch with Joey and his family. Make sure they're safe." He assured me he would, but Joey and Janet were out of town, on an isolated beach. They didn't even know what was happening. So my husband went to be with our grandsons, Ben and Dave, by then in their twenties, living on their own in Elon.

That entire day, I just didn't get it. Why didn't everyone see the implications? Why was everyone acting as if everything was normal? Would anything ever be normal again?

For a couple of days, I was so terrified that I jumped at every loud noise. Would there be other incidences? Would we ultimately be destroyed? Gradually I returned to an existence that was almost normal. I felt grateful to be alive, happy to do what I could for my father and brother. What did I have to complain about? I was alive, wasn't I?

After 9/11 I noticed a change in Greensboro. Suddenly people were even more open. Total strangers would grin broadly and say "hello." Fewer people were honking their horns as they drove down highways. For a few brief hours on an unfortunate day, the enemy had demonstrated how vunerable we were. And what did we do? We smiled at one another, gleeful to still be here, newly appreciating life.

Shagging At The Beach

Early on March 5, 2002, we received a phone. My son Mike had taken his wife Tina to the hospital in Georgetown to give birth to their first child. My eldest son's boys were now young men, so my husband and I were thrilled at the prospects of having a small grandchild once more, one that we could cuddle in our arms and watch as he or she discovered the wonderment of this world. My son hoped for a boy. Secretly, I longed for a girl.

My husband and I encountered fog as we headed to the coast. There had been a storm at sea the night before. As I drove, Joe dialed Mike on the cell phone. The baby was being born that minute, Mike said. He had to hang up. By the time we arrived, our granddaughter Amber had already joined us. Wrapped tightly in a receiving blanket, she resembled a burrito. Immediately we lost our heart to our tiny red-haired granddaughter. Now, at six, she owns it still.

Later, to commemorate Amber's arrival, I wrote an article for the *News & Record*, describing the morning following our granddaughter's birth. Rising early that day, we walked on Huntington Beach. How astonished Joe and I were when we saw hundreds of starfish covering the shore. My own belief was that the starfish had been sent by nature to greet our own little star, Amber Marie Redding. Evidently readers connected to the article I wrote. Several people commented on it. One woman sent me a lovely poem she'd written about her own grandchild.

Amber truly is sugar and spice. Though sweet and charming, she readily shares her opinions with all who wish to listen. By age three, she'd put her hands on her hips and let us know whether she agreed or disagreed with what we thought would be best for her. When she was five, she fell from the rings on her swing set and crashed into the side of a wagon below. The fall resulted in a broken arm. Though I often fear for her safety, I can't help but admire her adventuresome spirit.

Like both her mother and father, Amber loves sports. She enjoys watching football and basketball games, but she'd rather be personally involved. She swims like a fish and hits a soft ball with a high degree of accuracy. And, blessed with a bountiful imagination, she loves drawing pictures and telling stories.

When my granddaughter visits us in Greensboro, we play together. Sometimes we color or make beaded bracelets. We also enjoy picking flowers and arranging them. Every morning and every afternoon she prepares *pretend* tea for me; every evening we tell stories.

The summer of 2007, when she spent a week with us, my husband and I let Amber decide what to do. Because she wanted to see animals, particularly polar bears, we stopped at the North Carolina Zoo in Asheboro on our way back to Greensboro. It was a hot July day and she was tired out from the long trip. Still she enjoyed the apes and monkeys, calling the small monkey who looked at her from behind glass, "You silly thing." The elephants and giraffes were larger than anything she'd imagined, but she laughed with delight as she watched the antics of the polar bears. The colorful birds in the aviary, particularly the toucans, intrigued all of us, and at the end of our visit to the zoo, ice cream hit the spot. Guess what thrilled Amber most? The art spot, a garden area where kids were encouraged to paint pictures. She decided that the work of art she created that day would be a gift for her Mom.

During her stay, we allowed Amber to sleep as late as she wanted. I like to sleep late too. When she was ready for breakfast, Grandpop scrambled her cheese eggs just the way she liked them. Then we'd plan our day.

Amber has a fondness for critters that creep and crawl, so when she visits us, she always requests a visit to the Environmental Center. After the thrill of being allowed to hold a snake or lizard, she capers through the dinosaur exhibit and then shops for pretend groceries in the room set up like a grocery store and kitchen. On her last visit with us, the Environmental Center had completed an animal park outside. Amber teased the gibbons and was fascinated by the peacocks, their tails spread like colorful fans, as they preened for attention. The white tigers, even though kept behind a glass enclosure, intimidated both of us.

Playing with other children is always the most fun for our granddaughter, so we were pleased that we met up with Susan and Jim Varner, whom Joe and I had known since high school, and their two lovely granddaughters.

The Children's Museum, a treat for children of all ages, was at the top of our "to do" list the following day. Soon as we went inside, Amber scaled the wall. Next she hopped in the real fire truck, sounding all its bells and whistles. There was so much for her to see and enjoy, but best of all was the art corner, where she could paint pictures.

My husband and I freeze stale bread, saving it for Amber's visits. Every afternoon she demanded that we take her to the Bog Garden to feed ducks. While there, she also enjoys searching for turtles, frogs, and fish. Another Greensboro ritual is going to Maxie B's on Battleground for ice cream. She considers it to be the coolest ice cream parlor she's ever seen. I agree.

Maxie B's on Battleground Avenue was named for the beloved pet dog of the owner. The cozily elegant décor inside features sofas covered in animal prints, a chandelier, and in the bathroom, gold fixtures. Fresh flowers center each table and if you don't care for ice cream or yogurt, Maxi B's also serves delicious cakes. The humming bird cake is a personal favorite, but Amber always opts for one scoop of crazy vanilla ice cream covered with sprinkles and served in a dish. Yum. Yum.

On the day before Amber left going back to Myrtle Beach, she threw a party for her grandpop. She'd earned the money to buy balloons, cupcakes, ice cream and butterfly stickers to stick to napkins by being a "good girl" all week.

When she visited in the fall, my husband and I introduced our granddaughter to the Barnum and Bailey Circus, a Redding tradition. My friend Anne Barnhill, who now lives in Garner, and her blue-eyed granddaughter Virginia joined us. The girls nibbled popcorn as they viewed the daredevil attempts of cyclists speeding inside a ball-shaped enclosure, and trapeze artists, sailing through the air, but not necessarily with the greatest of ease. One of them grimaced. Of course, the girls were amused by the clowns and animals, particularly the prancing horses. But the elephants got top billing. When we asked what they liked best, they giggled, and then Amber answered: "All the elephant poop."

This year, during the week of July 4th, our granddaughter once again got together with Virginia Smith. After having lunch and playing games at Chucky Cheese, they spent the afternoon at the Natural Science Center. Virginia, always sweet and considerate, brought Amber a ladybug ring and invited her to join her ladybug club. My hope is that Amber and Virginia will remain ladybug friends forever.

The next day, at ArtQuest, a children's program located in the Cultural Arts Center in downtown Greensboro, Amber lived out her dream by making art for one entire afternoon. She worked with clay, paint, cutouts, and fabrics and yarn. I've never seen her happier. Then, on the Fourth of July, we celebrated by watching the fantastic Bicentennial parade downtown and drinking lemonade. In the afternoon we walked up to the Kirkwood parade that's become a neighborhood tradition. Amber, determined to get candy, waved a flag and smiled. She also shouted out "Happy Fourth of July" to everyone and told the politicians, "I voted for you." The candy rained down from the floats, trucks and cars. Such a sweet monsoon.

I hope my beautiful granddaughter with the strawberry blond hair will visit us often. The next time she comes to Greensboro, I plan to take her on a tour of the University of North Carolina here. Wouldn't it be grand if some day she decided she wanted to attend my alma mater?

FAMILY FINALE

Every dance must end; so must every life. We long for the closing stages of both dances and lives to be graceful. Most dances do end with a satisfying conclusion. But death, even an expected death, usually takes those watching by surprise. Thus, we are denied a stirring climatic moment, some word or gesture to sweeten our memories of the loved one's last moments.

The first few months after mother died, I'd panic whenever my father hit a rough spot, particularly if he needed to be hospitalized. During the four years my father spent at Cross Road, he survived several episodes of severe illness. In 2000, he suffered a heart attack which required that a stint be inserted into an artery that was over 90 per cent closed. While the doctors worked to repair his heart, he shocked the entire medical team by standing up on the operating table. A year later, he fell, breaking his hip. As I sat with him in the hospital, I feared he wouldn't survive but, miraculously, he not only lived through the ordeal, but learned to walk again, a truly amazing feat for someone with Alzheimer's.

My father survived for several years, despite Alzheimer's, which is not unusual. Tragically it's often the caregiver who dies first. Medical studies confirm that the stress of witnessing a loved one sink away can be deadly. That, I believe, is what happened to my mother. Though her death certificate specified liver cancer, her unwillingness to seek early medical help and stress due to my father's illness were probably the actual culprits. Though I vowed that I would not follow a similar path, in July of 2002, I became quite ill while with my husband in Reading, Pennsylvania. I had violent chest pains and felt so weak I could barely stand, still I adamantly refused to go to the hospital in Reading, so after a sleepless night, my husband drove me back to Greensboro. Being sick is never a pleasant experience, but being sick and away from home is enough to induce a major stress attack.

The *Welcome to Greensboro* sign was absolutely the prettiest sight I'd ever seen. Pushing the gas pedal, my husband sped to Moses Cone Hospital. After a three-hour wait, they finally began their prodding and testing. Finally, after I pleaded for mercy, they gave me a shot to ease pain. The verdict: Gall stones had caused an infection. I'd need surgery.

The surgeon who examined me in the hospital scheduled my operation for several days later. The next day, in a great deal of pain, I decided I couldn't wait that long, so I called my primary physician, Dr. Annemarie Mazzocchi, one of the wisest women I know. She recommended Dr. Patrick Ballen, who agreed to see me that afternoon. A truly compassionate doctor, he removed my diseased gall bladder the following morning at Wesley Long Hospital.

During that time I worried about my father and brother.

What if something happened to them while I was recovering? Despite my trepidations, Dr. Ballen and the hospital nurses took excellent care of me and by the next afternoon I returned home.

My brother called, letting me know that he'd been deeply concerned over my illness. Once again, I tried convincing him that it might be easier for everyone if both he and Dad were in Greensboro. We'd already found out that Dad could no longer stay at Cross Road because his insurance required more nursing care than could be provided there, so I moved him to Evergreens, located just off Wendover Avenue. Mick, for a while, considered moving into a condo in Greensboro, but ultimately changed his mind.

In 2002, my husband took a photograph that came to mean a great deal to me. My youngest son and his family had visited us during the Christmas season. Amber, at the time, was only eight months old. We took her to see Dad at Evergreens, and, while there, Joe took a photo of the four generations—Dad, me, my son Mike, and my granddaughter. It's the only picture I have of Amber with my father. As I posed for the picture my heart felt heavy, for I recalled that Mom died before Amber's birth. How she would have loved my beautiful granddaughter, who, like her, had Marie for her middle name.

Shortly after Christmas of 2002, I received a call from Evergreens. Dad had pneumonia. They were taking him to Cone Hospital. Used to such calls, I didn't panic.

As I drove to Cone Hospital, I recalled how pale my father had looked during my last visit, two days before. That day, in spite of my urging, he only ate a bit of bread and a couple of spoonfuls of applesauce. Still, he'd always bounced back before. Surely he'd do so again.

When I asked the receptionist at Cone for my father's room number, she couldn't find him listed. When I explained the situation in great detail, she said, not to worry, he was probably still in the emergency room. When she called there, they said they had no record of my father being admitted.

As I headed for the administration office, I could feel my heart pounding. After I explained my predicament to an intelligent looking woman, she said, don't worry, they probably took your father back to Evergreen. She picked up the phone to call them.

Dad was not at Evergreen, and they were certain he'd been taken to the emergency room at Moses Cone Hospital. By that time I'd pushed a panic button and so had the smiling woman in administration. She called the emergency room, her voice gritty with determination. She would stay on the line, she said, until they found Elmer Raby. I bit my lip, attempting to hold back tears. Had my father managed to get up off the gurney and walked away? Perhaps, he'd died on the way to the hospital. Could they have already taken him to the morgue?

Finally, after waiting several minutes, bracing myself for the worse, I was given an answer. When my father was taken to the emergency room at Cone, they had no room for him, so the ambulance carried him to Wesley Long. I was assured that my father could be found there.

By that time I was in an "I'll believe it when I see it" frame of mind. After driving to Wesley Long, I rushed into the emergency room, demanding that I see Dad. When finally I got to him, he didn't look like my father at all. Despite the Alzheimer's, the heart attack, and the hip fracture, my father had still looked hearty and strong. Now, suddenly, he seemed diminished. He was finding it difficult to breathe, even with an oxygen mask. When

I said, "Daddy," he opened his eyes. In them, I saw fear.

He remained in the hospital over two weeks, his breathing labored and noisy. When Mom was still alive, we had agreed as a family that no extraordinary measures would be made to keep my father alive when he eventually faced a life-threatening situation. There would be no feeding shunt; he would not be hooked up to machines. He would not have wanted it.

When the doctor said that it was probably just a matter of time, I called my brother. "Don't you want to come up here?" I asked. "Joe will come for you."

My brother insisted he was too ill to come. The cold weather had caused his arthritis to flair up, becoming ever more unbearable. His doctor had increased the pain medication, but, even so, he found it almost impossible to get out of bed. Maybe, by the weekend, he said, he'd feel well enough to make the trip.

The next day my father continued to make agonizing noises, attempting to breathe. His doctor came into the room to examine him. Putting the ends of the stethoscope in his ears, he placed the metal disc on my father's back to listen to his lungs. My father surprised all of us. His head popped up and his eyes opened. "Get that God damned piece of ice off me." he shouted.

The doctor looked positively stunned. I laughed, thinking Oh, Daddy, then wondered what it meant. Was my father recovering? The doctor, though surprised by my father's vigor, discouraged our optimism. Dad's vital signs were no stronger. I remembered that my mother believed that women, just before they had babies, as well as older people, just before they died, had sudden surges of energy.

The next night, one week after New Year's Day 2003, my father died.

The funeral service was held at Pugh Funeral Home in Randleman, the small town my father loved. Many people he'd worked with showed up and some of my friends from Greensboro came as well. I deeply appreciated their presence. David Schwartz, who'd been so good to Daddy at Cross Road, had charge of the service. He brought a soft ball, the one that Mick and I had tossed back and forth to Daddy to help him retain motor skills. The three of us had also tossed the ball to Penny, the Irish setter that stayed at Cross Road, providing companionship for the residents. David considered our tossing the ball back and forth to be a game of connection. After the service, Dad was carried to Randolph Memorial Garden in Asheboro, where he was buried beside Mom.

The next few months were particularly difficult for my brother. With the help of my husband and son, I eventually cleared everything out of the huge attic upstairs in Mom and Dad's house. Mick and I sorted through each item, carefully considering what must be done with it. Many items had been ruined. Some we gave to friends who would appreciate them or to Goodwill.

My mother, bless her heart, had been a hoarder. Having lived through the depression, she believed every object had dual purposes. For example, she boxed up discarded nylon stockings, believing that someone might use them to tie up Vidalia onions and hang them from the ceiling, thus delaying deterioration. She also saved huge boxes of discarded looper clips my father had brought home from the mill. Maybe, someday, she believed, she would make potholders out of them. The uniforms my brother had worn while in the Air Force were there, as well as a yellowed evening gown I'd worn in high school. Stacks of *Look* magazines, some of them dating back to the early 1950's, lay crumbled by time, in one corner.

When we finally finished cleaning the attic and organizing closets and drawers, I helped my brother move his possessions from the garage apartment into the larger house. Then, together, we planned possible renovations.

Because of Mick's health, all these changes went very slow. He spent many hours resting. Time was also put aside for his art work, genealogy and writing. His paintings and collages were quite striking. I treasure the pieces I've kept. He'd worked on the genealogy for a number of years. He also gathered all the old family photos and placed them in albums. Like me, my brother enjoyed writing. He'd had several articles and reviews published when he lived in Atlanta.

After my father died, I took some time to catch up with the world beyond family. I didn't like what I read and saw. Angry at President Bush's insistence that troops be sent to Iraq, I briefly became an activist.

When George Bush first began talking about war in Iraq, my blood ran cold. How could we be so advanced as a society and still believe that differences could be resolved by killing people? I was absolutely enraged when it became clear that he planned to go on with war plans without the approval of the United Nations. I signed petitions. I went with my friend Anne Barnhill to the office of Representative Richard Burr to protest. I went with my friend Sharin Francis to a concert at Guilford College featuring musicians advocating peace.

Though, at the time, my tiny cry for peace seemed merely a gut reaction to President Bush's inane war policy, I later discovered that while focusing on peace for the world, I attained an inner peace that helped me deal with what lay ahead. Presently I continue to explore various meditations and other methods of staying calm. Recently I joined a drum circle, and later this year, I intend to hold a dance for peace.

My brother's illness remained, in many ways, a mystery to me. Always a private person, he informed the family of only the bare bones of his condition. He kept his regular doctor appointments, but never allowed anyone to accompany him into the doctor's office. From time to time, he would complain about one medication or another. He'd laugh, as if telling a joke, and inform me that he'd had to stop taking a particular medication. "They've found out it kills people" was always the macabre punch line.

In truth, my brother's condition worsened, in part, because of the decisions he made. He'd been told early on how important exercise was, particularly aquatic exercise, yet he never went to a pool. I suppose he dreaded parading his bent body before others.

By the summer of 2002, it was apparent that my brother's health was on a descending spiral. I pleaded with him to be more aggressive. If he needed physical therapy, I'd take him wherever he needed to go. Though I didn't realize it then, there was something else going on, a new medical problem.

Though Mick could have gotten Meals on Wheels, he didn't want to do so. So in addition to taking him to the doctor and picking up his prescriptions and groceries, I began doing some cooking for him, laundered his clothes, and cleaned his house once a week. In retrospect, that was darned generous of me, for, I've never been fond of chasing dust bunnies.

Realizing that my brother was losing ground, I worried about him constantly. What if he fell? I made him promise to always carry his cell phone with him. In many ways, he was just as concerned about me. I'd had my gall bladder removed, he reminded me. I needed to be more careful about my diet. He also spoke of the dangers of stress. I knew I wasn't immune. They say that blood pressure is the silent killer, because we're unaware if our blood pressure rises. But I knew when mine shot up; I could feel it.

One October night that year, the phone rang in the middle of the night. It was Mick. He needed me to come pick him up.

"Where are you?" I asked, feeling my blood pressure soar.

"In the emergency room at Cone Hospital," he said. "They've discharged me. I'm ready to go home."

"How did you get there?"

"I called 911."

Why had he not called me, I wondered as I sped to the emergency room. When I arrived, my brother attempted to assure me he was okay, but the lie was obvious. His face was drawn and weary. He explained that he'd been dehydrated, so they'd hooked him up to an IV.

But what caused it? I pressured him.

He'd felt that he might pass out, he said. He'd been unable to eat anything. He had something inside his mouth, maybe a canker sore.

I wasn't buying it. After taking him home, I spent the night there, in the house where I'd grown up. As I slept, family ghosts inhabited my dreams, all of them telling me that I must help my brother. The next morning I dialed Mick's doctor in Greensboro, insisting that he see my brother right away. Then I went to Mick's bedroom and demanded that he get dressed.

I ardently believe in individual rights, but my nerves could no long endure the mystery of my brother's illness. That day I boldly followed him into the doctor's office. Soon as the nurse looked inside my brother's mouth, she headed for the doctor. After his examination, the doctor looked mystified. "I'm making an appointment for you with an oral surgeon," he said.

Later that morning, as we waited in Dr. Newman's office, I looked at my brother, trying to gauge what might be going on inside his head. When the doctor came in, he instructed Mick to open his mouth. I saw the problem then: a worm-shaped growth on the left side of his tongue. I remembered the MRI of the tumor on Mom's liver. The shape on Mick's tongue was similar. I wasn't surprised when Dr. Newman explained that it looked like cancer. When the doctor left the room to make arrangements for further tests, I felt as if I couldn't breathe. My brother's face was pale as paste. He opened his brown eyes, studying me. "Don't be sad, Sandra," he said. "This might be a way out for me."

The next month was agony for all of us. Mick had to have all his teeth removed. To get rid of the cancer his entire tongue would need to be removed. Dr. Newman didn't advocate such drastic surgery, and it wasn't what my brother wished either. He tried radiation treatments but they were pure torture for him because of his distorted body. When he could no longer eat, inserting a shunt for food was suggested. My brother refused. After talking with my brother, one of the hospital psychiatrists explained to me that because the quality of his life had dramatically diminished, Mick didn't wish any measures to be taken to prolong living. A saline drip containing morphine was inserted. He lived for four more days. Two days before Christmas of 2003, he died as I held his hand. The service was held the day after Christmas. Because my brother served in the Air Force during the Viet Nam era, his casket was draped with a flag. I recalled the burials of three of my uncles, all veterans of World War II. His resting place, at the feet of my mother and father, is in the family plot at Memorial Garden in Asheboro.

SWINGING TO A LIVELIER BEAT

Even now, just thinking of the last few weeks of my brother's life makes my heart hurt. Extremely intelligent, he was blessed with many talents. Yet, because of illness, there was so much he could no longer manage. I recall a question the psychiatrist asked my brother: If you enjoyed good health what would your life be like? My brother said he would travel, he would attend concerts and plays, and he would write.

Fortunately, I did have good health. And the desires my brother expressed were open to me. But at the very top of my list was spending more time with my husband.

While Joe and I walked on the Peninsula Trail in Greensboro one Sunday morning, dancing beams of sunlight filtered through the canopy of leaves above us. I stood there entranced. Perhaps Mick was telling me something, I decided. Maybe, he's sending down a blessing, letting me know that he approves my being outside and enjoying the woods, something he hadn't been able to do for nearly forty years. Then another thought occurred to me, I would honor my brother and my father and mother by living the best possible life. I felt sure they would be pleased, for they had constantly reminded me of the importance of looking after my own health.

2004 was a busy year. Besides teaching and working on temporary assignments at Measurement, I had to look after the sale of my parent's house in Randleman and also settle my brother's estate. There was much work needed to get the house ready. But I knew I would have help. As always, my husband pitched in. What began as a dance of frustration soon became a smooth glide of togetherness as we worked side by side to achieve our goal of selling the house by the end of the year. Our son Joey was also a tremendous help, bringing his expertise as a building contractor to the team effort. He renovated the bathroom, fixed a leak in the roof, and brought physical strength and intelligence to projects that couldn't have been completed without him. Our grandson David, an excellent painter, even came down a couple of Saturdays, lending a hand. But, as always, it was my industrious husband I relied on most.

Painting is always a necessity if getting ready to sell. I actually enjoyed that task. While painting the interior, I meditated, freeing my mind of everything except the repetitive brush strokes needed to transform a worn ugly wall into something clean and new. Spending hours on landscaping, my husband mowed, weeded and planted colorful flowers in my mother's beloved garden.

I also relied on the valuable counsel of Frank Wells, a wise compassionate attorney, who helped me sort out the entanglements of my brother's estate. Kudos, too, for Grace Steed, a Randleman realtor, who provided ample advice and professional assistance as I came to terms with selling the home where I'd grown up, a place filled with family memories.

After putting the house on the market, we held a large tag and yard sale. In addition to advertising in the newspaper, I hand carried notices to everyone in the neighborhood. I loved that friends and neighbors of my mother, father, and brother showed up that crisp October day. Because Mother had been quite the collector, several antique dealers dropped by, anxious to purchase family treasures, such as the sideboard that had always sat in the dining room or the ancient trunks, holding quilts made by my grandmother.

In October, 2004, after closing on the sale of the house that had belonged to my parents, I finally relaxed for the first time in a long while. Realizing that the years were rushing by, fast as a bullet train, I reclaimed my life.

The previous Christmas had been impossibly sad because my brother had died only two days before, but we celebrated Christmas of 2004 with renewed vigor, relishing the antics of our two-year-old granddaughter Amber. My husband and I prepared to kick off 2005 by making reservations at the Barn Dinner Theater, located on Stage Coach Trail in Greensboro, for our New Year's Eve celebration. Over the years, we'd been there many times, often with friends, and we were always pleased with both the buffet and the performance. The Barn Dinner Theatre has long been a first- class destination for a relaxing evening of laughter and fun. Our favorite play of all the ones we've seen there is *Smoke on the Mountain*, a light-hearted look at a small church congregation. Filled with gospel music, cornball humor, and a mother lode of good will, the actors bring to life a slice of rural North Carolina that's only slightly exaggerated.

Our Barn experience on New Year's Eve 2005, began with dinner. As usual, the buffet tables groaned beneath platters of delectable food. Once again the halibut was prepared just right. The crowd roared when the featured performer, Stephen Freeman, a talented Elvis Pressley tribute artist, took the stage. Once with the High Point Police Department, Stephen now entertains throughout the country, always drawing huge crowds. Though not as tall as Elvis (nor as stout), when the lights dim, I swear he becomes "The King". His voice is so similar it's uncanny. Grandmothers went wild that night, begging him to place one of the white scarves he carried around their neck or give them a kiss. Going to a Stephen Freeman performance is Las Vegas without slot machines.

After the performance, champagne was served and dance music began. That evening was particularly memorable to me, for my husband danced with me several times. Though dancing makes him uncomfortable, I can think of only a few things I'd rather do. I love swing and the cha-cha. But a waltz or foxtrot is fun too. Free style's probably my favorite, just getting up and shaking away inhibitions.

Just before midnight, waitresses distributed horns and hats and a huge roar erupted as we shouted in 2005. After breakfast, we left, ready to face whatever the year might hold.

During that year, I began to write in earnest again. I had a million projects in mind. How would I complete all of them? Like dance, writing required a plan. After a great deal of thought, I settled down to a four-hours-per-day work schedule, determined to complete a novel that I had begun before the pressure of family illnesses left no time for it. While my family members were so sick, my mind became consumed with whatever I needed to do to make them more comfortable. I did some writing, but the passion required to complete a book had evaporated. Now, finally, I joyfully dedicated myself to the task of putting words on paper again. I make no claims about my expertise as a writer, but I can state unequivocally that nothing gives me more pleasure. Well, perhaps dancing.

I also wrote a few articles that were published that year and I regularly wrote a column for the *News&Record*, my home town newspaper, in which I reviewed books by North Carolina authors. Elma Sebo, my editor, was a delight to work with. I admired her professionalism and her enthusiasm for books and authors. Few writing experiences are more satisfying for me than discovering a first-time author who has written a magical book, then sharing that experience with readers. Several times that happened while writing reviews for newspapers and magazines. Just two years ago, I wrote a glowing review of a book by Sarah Addison Allen, a young woman from Asheville. How gratifying when I discovered later that the book has been included on the New York Times bestseller list. Now Sarah has published her second magical realism novel, *The Sugar Queen*. Having recently finished reading it, I proclaim her future to be shiny with possibility.

North Carolina, in general, and Greensboro, in particular, is fertile ground for writers. So many fine novelists, poets and journalists sojourn here. Thus, for anyone aspiring to be a writer, it's a fortuitous place. A discovery by my husband, an avid reader of mystery and suspense books, was John Hart, who now lives in Greensboro. After hearing Hart read at Barnes & Noble, I purchased his first mystery, *King of Lies*, for Joe. He found it to be a mesmerizing book. At a recent reading the author mentioned that his book has been optioned by a motion picture producer. Touted by many to be the next John Grisham, John Hart now has a second book out and is writing a third.

For readers, many resources exist in Greensboro. Barnes & Noble booksellers host readings, featuring both local and nationally known writers. Becky Carignan, Community Relations Manager of the local book store, personally knows most of the local writers and actively keeps patrons informed of upcoming readings. Another large bookstore, Borders, is located on High Point Road. Though I'm fond of Borders, I don't get there too frequently. Barnes & Noble at Friendly Shopping Center happens to be closer to my doorstep.

The public library also does a bang-up job of keeping the public informed. Beth Sheffield, who heads up the Reader's Advisory Service at the central library located on North Church Street, regularly plans lunch and read series to entice the public. For readers interested in poetry, Steve Sumerford, Assistant Director of the library, plans a bevy of activities throughout the year. In April, designated Poetry Month in Greensboro, the library sponsors a reading by a major poet. Last year Nikki Giovanni was featured. Steve also spearheaded the idea of having poetry readings in local coffee shops and bringing the great gift of poetry to senior citizens with by having volunteers conduct workshops in local retirement homes and rehabilitation facilities.

The readings and workshops at area universities and colleges are another rich resource for those who love words. The Creative Writing program at the University of North Carolina in Greensboro offers frequent readings, free and open to the public. The program also sponsors a yearly small magazine and press conference, giving writers an opportunity to meet and chat with editors who might take an interest in their work.

Several area writers' organizations also exist locally. I've been the grateful recipient of advice and encouragement from the Writer's Group of the Triad in Greensboro and the North Carolina Writer's Network, presently a virtual resource, assessed by computer.

Dancing Here, Dancing There, Dancing Everywhere

After my brother died, it took a while for me to believe it was okay to have fun. While caring for him and my parents, I'd missed traveling to new placing. Still, even then, my husband Joe and I took time to go to Myrtle Beach every two or three months to spend time with our youngest son and his family. But, often, on these quick weekend family jaunts, no time remained to gaze at the ocean or to explore new areas of the South Carolina coast. And when we made those hurry-up trips, I always remained anxious and concerned over the sick members of my family I'd left behind. What if they needed to be hospitalized while I was gone? What if they had a new medical problem but hadn't let me know for fear of ruining my trip?

Before my family members became ill, I'd loved the prospect of exploring new terrain. Over the years, my husband and I enjoyed several memorable trips. Our favorite: Hawaii, where we traveled when our son Michael was in High School. During the trip, we fell in love with the roar of the ocean on isolated beaches, the gentle smiles of natives, and the scent of flowers everywhere. We savored the food, the music, the myths and legends and the diversity celebrated at the Polynesian Village. While there, I posed for a photograph with Don Ho, the entertainer who made "Tiny Bubbles" famous, and Joe posed for snapshots with the lovely Hula girls at the Kodak Center.

On another trip, we enjoyed the different cultures of New Mexico, evidenced in the art, food, and entertainment of that eclectic state. Arizona, too, amazed us, the terrain so different from our own. And New Orleans, what fun! We especially enjoyed a boat trip down a swamp just outside the city. Alligators everywhere! Later, when we viewed on television the damage wrought by Hurricane Katrina, we were grateful that we'd toured the fun city, filled with music and dance, during its glory days.

We'd also explored Florida and most of the Southeast. Once, after receiving my B.A. in English, I completed my education by traveling in England and France. And while Joe and I were in Arizona, we'd gone over the border for a quick trip to Mexico.

Still there was so much we hadn't seen, and by 2005 I felt ready to Hip Hop here, there, everywhere.

In July, 2004, soon after hanging up my caregiver coat, my husband and I rented a car at the Rhode Island airport and we took off, eager to explore New England. I particularly enjoyed seeing Stowe, Vermont that week. It's a lovely area even when the ski slopes aren't in operation. We hiked through the woods where *The Sound of Music* was filmed and visited the Ben & Jerry factory for a tour and free samples.

During the trip we were also in New Hampshire, noted for its rugged White Mountains, part of the Appalachian range. When we reached Bangor, Maine, we headed for Acadia National Park, a spectacular vision of tall mountains lumbering over a turbulent sea. Unfortunately the weather turned damp while we were there, so we missed the spectacular sunrise that Jenna Bush, George Bush's daughter, spoke of seeing the morning her fiancé proposed. Maine is beautiful but startling. Moose Crossing signs are posted along the highway, and hunters are cautioned not to shoot game from a truck bed.

In Connecticut, we avoided the casinos. Instead we enjoyed Mystic Seaport, a living museum that covers over 17 acres, depicting coastal life in New England in the 19th century. What fun to walk about talking to folks dressed as sea captains and craftsmen, explaining how everything was made and run more than a hundred years before.

As fun as the trip had been, once we got back home, we decided again that no matter how far we traveled, we'd probably never find a place that pleased us more than Greensboro. Here, as in Massachusetts, we have a strong sense of history and a deep appreciation for literature. Massachusetts has Nathaniel Hawthorne's home, the intriguing Seven Gables. But we have the interesting boarding house that belonged to Thomas Wolfe's mother, only a few hours away in Asheville. Lilacs here don't grow nearly as tall as those in New England. I've heard that growth there results from cold winters. I certainly don't envy New Englanders their ice and snow. I do suppose, though, that's why so many Dunking Doughnut shops are found in that area. Still, we have Krispy Crème, the doughnut dynasty the first began in nearby Winston Salem, and recently Dunking Doughnut actually opened a shop in Greensboro.

Though glad to be home, I noticed how much my husband and I had neglected our own home. All my efforts at been directed to getting the house in Randleman ready to sell. Now that we'd escaped day-to-day realities for a bit, it was time to update our own place. Finally feeling up to the task, I was ready to rock 'n roll.

Having several unhealthy trees cut down and others trimmed improved the landscape. My husband drew up plans for a new deck. After the deck was completed, we replaced the old fence. Wherever we've lived, Joe has always made sure we had azaleas and dogwood trees. We also keep a small rose garden. The Big Boy and German Johnson tomatoes he grew became the crowning glory of the back yard.

My son Joey, quite a craftsman, made a Zen bench for my birthday a few years ago. We placed it in a shady corner of our backyard. I piled crystal rocks I'd rescued from my parents yard in a circle, filling in with small stones in that area. My husband added a rhododendron bush and used periwinkle for ground cover. In 2007, I added another gift from my son and his wife Janet to the area. The Bird Girl, a reproduction of the one in the Savannah Georgia Art Museum and featured in the movie, *Midnight in the Garden of Good and Evil*, adds just the right touch to the serene garden.

Joey built a large flowerbox for his father, which we placed on the rebuilt deck. When he brought it to us, I joked that it was large as a coffin. He also built a couple of wooden tables for plants and a potting table. When we sit outside on balmy days, I'm always grateful for my son's handiwork. My grandfather worked for Tomlinson, a furniture manufacturer in High Point, North Carolina, as did three of my uncles. They were master craftsmen in their day. I still have a small stool, which I treasure, made for me by my Grandfather, Thomas Jetter Butler. My son must have inherited craftsmen's genes from him.

Work on the inside of the house began in 2005. That spring we painted several rooms and, again with the help of our son, renovated the kitchen. We depended on Lowe's, located on Battleground Road, to help us select the needed materials. They guided us as we selected appliances, countertops, and cabinet fronts. I spoke to my son of the vision I had and, miraculously, he made it happen for a reasonable cost. Mostly my husband and I agreed, but he wanted a tile floor and I opted for a laminated one, believing it would make the room appear larger and add warmth. Though he likes the kitchen, he's still not fond of the floor.

I made a vow that year that no matter how busy we might be with work, nor how much we enjoyed just being at home, I didn't want to get stuck in a rut. Though in my mid-sixties, I still wanted to learn. I also wanted to be entertained. There were so many places I'd never seen. Before I bit the dust, I vowed, I'd get to every state.

In May, Doug and Ione Woodlief talked us into going to Las Vegas with them. Las Vegas wasn't a place Joe and I would have chosen without some arm twisting, because while in the Bahamas, the casinos had frightened us. How foolish people could be, we thought, gambling hours away when they could be outside exploring the beaches or woods.

Actually, though, we had a great time in Las Vegas. We enjoyed traveling with our friends, especially since they'd been there and knew what we should be sure to see. There's a gaudy overkill to the strip that transforms Vegas into a grown-up version of Disney World. Still, there's no better place to people watch.

A highlight was attending the featured Cirque du Soliel show at the Ballagio Casino. As we watched in awe, the troupe performed graceful dance moves and incredible acts of daring above and in the water. The humor, tricks of illusion, and sheer artistry of the spectacle provided us with an enchanting evening.

As always, we relish time spent with the Woodliefs, whether vacationing, dining at local restaurants such as Bianca's or Elizabeth's, or driving up to Shatley Springs, located in the foothills, for a country-style meal. For such excursions, Doug insists on being behind the wheel of his car. I've never known anyone who loved driving more. When Joe and I get into the back seat of his sedan, we realize that we might end up in Virginia or Tennessee before the sun sets.

Having always been fond of dance, I was easily drawn to the Folkmoot USA, the international dance festival celebrated in the mountains of Western North Carolina each summer. In Waynesville, over 300 performers gather from a dozen or more countries to perform cultural dances in colorful costumes. In July 2005, I talked my husband into going. We enjoyed the parade in Waynesville. The next evening, we attended one of the many performances held throughout the area during the two-week event. The one we selected took place at the University of North Carolina in Asheville. Troupes from each country performed both a folk dance and a wedding dance. I sat there, enthralled. This summer, July 14-27, 2008, the Folkmoot will celebrate its 25th year in the beautiful mountains of North Carolina.

Our last opportunity to get away in 2005 was a working vacation in October. Joe and I had an opportunity to go to Wildacres, located near the Blue Ridge Parkway. The climb is on a narrow road, not all of it paved. But once there, you are reminded that, in autumn, everyone should go to the mountains for great gulps of tranquility and to view one of nature's most spectacular performances, the color of tree leaves changing to vibrant yellows, oranges, reds, and purples. There's nothing quite like the majesty of North Carolina's mountains to restore one's soul.

Wildacres is a retreat owned by the Blumenthal family. I'd been there several times for writing workshops, but having my husband with me made that trip even more special. Joe took photographs while I worked on editing a novel I'd been working on for years. When not working, we visited the potters, painters, jewelry designers, and musicians who were also attending. Some afternoons, we simply sat in rocking chairs, drinking in incredible mountain vistas.

By December we agreed that we'd had a pretty fabulous year. I sipped Chardonnay while my husband downed a Corona. We promised ourselves that 2006 would be just as great.

The Twist

2005 and 2006 were years of remembrance.

In 2005, I attended my Randleman High School class reunion at the Asheboro Country Club in Randolph County. After receiving an invitation, I struggled to remember each and every face of those I'd graduated with in 1957. For the occasion, I wore a purple dress, one that I'd purchased the year before to wear to the wedding of Bree Lovatt, the beautiful daughter of my friend Kathryn, who for many years lived in Greensboro. Now Kathryn and her husband Dan live in South Carolina but travel back to the "green" city several times a year. Their son Xan attends Guilford College.

As Joe and I rode to the reunion, I had nothing but sterling memories of my classmates. They were all fine folks and I'd learned valuable lessons from many of them as well as my teachers. But, when spotting two familiar faces after we walked in the door, another memory, one less sterling, flashed through my mind.

In 1956, our junior class had the responsibility of entertaining the seniors at a banquet. After careful consideration, a committee decided that the perfect place for the celebration was a clubhouse in Greensboro, an attractive house belonging to the Greensboro Woman's Club. The evening of the banquet, I wore my first strapless dress, a long white frilly gown, with a hoop beneath to make the skirt poof out. I dated Tommy Heath, a talented young classmate who loved teasing everyone. Joe, the man I later married, and his date, Barbara Parrish, an intelligent young woman who loved riding horses, went with us.

That evening we sipped ginger ale punch and enjoyed superb food served on fine china. Wearing silver high heel shoes and earrings fashioned from white feathers and rhinestones, I felt special. Our banquet theme, *Memories are Made of This,* included a display of pictures of my Junior and Senior classmates. After dinner, we chatted, laughed, and swayed romantically to popular tunes.

During the rest of the weekend, I remained in a cloud of teenage high spirits as I relived every moment of the banquet. But by Monday afternoon, my Pollyanna view of my classmates vanished.

Members of the Junior Class were called to the school auditorium. There had been complaints. The school's petite business teacher spoke to us in a no-nonsense voice. Many items, including silverware and salt shakers, were missing from the Woman's Clubhouse, and she knew we were responsible. Everything taken had to be returned, all of them. She would bring a pick-up truck to school the following day and if every single item wasn't returned, she's deal with us. From her demeanor everyone knew that she meant it.

Though I hate sounding like a goody two-shoes, I didn't steal a single item, honest. But there were several classmates I suspected. And what if they didn't return the items? Would the entire class have to share their penalty? Despite my pestering worries, the missing items must have been returned, for the incident was never mentioned again.

The teacher who'd always kept us honest didn't attend the class reunion. Both my husband and I had hopes she would. We had admired and learned from her, and in truth, she was never angry, except when she needed to be. Only one teacher, Adrian Neal, attended. Though he'd been rather quiet and conservative while teaching, he now loved telling jokes. When introduced, he stood up, entertaining us with anecdotes for several minutes.

Why was the reunion so important to me?

I always enjoy a good party, and I knew my talented peers on the reunion committee would make sure we had great food, decorations, and entertainment. I wasn't disappointed. Another reason attending mattered was curiosity. What had my classmates made of their lives? Were they well and were they happy?

Despite those who could not or chose not to come, the reunion turned out to be a joyous success. The dining area was filled with lovely flowers. The thoughtful committee had—thank you, thank you—dimmed the lights, so wrinkles weren't as visable. Stories from the past were recalled and good wishes for a blessed future bestowed. Perky Deeann Julian had arranged for a jukebox to be in the lobby, playing 1950's songs, including *Unchained Melody* and *Rock Around the Clock*.

That evening, I talked to practically everyone, including Larry "Rusty" Hammond, who, like me, had grown up on High Point Street in Randleman. Now, living in Asheboro, he's been a successful attorney and judge. What fun sharing old times and absorbing, in a brief space of time, as much as I could of the varied lives my former classmates had led.

Could the evening have been more perfect? Our class graduated in 1957, a gentle time. The President of the United States was Dwight Eisenhower, a former General, and schools were still segregated. Despite our conservative upbringing, it would have been interesting to pretend we'd attended Randleman High School a few years later. Then, perhaps, dancing and shouting would have been part of the plan. What fun twisting the night away might have been.

Before leaving the lovely country club, I had a revelation. I realized that though I'd made many missteps along my own path, I was actually pleased with how my life had turned out. I'd been blessed with a great family. And though the timing for my choices hadn't always been fine tuned, I'd still been able to pursue the education and profession I desired. And for most of those years, I'd lived happily in Greensboro, the city of my heart: a place I understood; a place that understood me.

The next year, my husband took his own trip to the past when making plans for his class reunion.

Joe, and other members of the 1956 Randleman High School reunion committee, began their preparations by contacting classmates to get addresses for the invitations. Reaching a dead end when trying to find a former student named Jack Hill, Doug Woodlief offered a brilliant suggestion. Why don't we go to Randleman and start knocking on doors, he asked my husband. Randleman's a small town. Surely, someone would know where Jack might be. Remarkably, someone did and the committee sent Jack an invitation to the Texas address they'd been given.

When the committee heard that Jack Hill wouldn't be coming, they were disappointed, but later, changing his mind, he surprised everyone, showing up with his wife Star, both of them wearing jeans and cowboy hats.

Joe also requested that class members send him current family photographs. Combining those with pictures from the high school annual, he produced a before and after video presentation that included everyone. Carrying out the Hawaiian theme, colorful leis and seashells decorated each table.

Bill Poe, who'd been class President, and his wife Nancy, everybody's favorite cheerleader, traveled from their home at the coast to attend. Elated to see our good friends again, we recalled many of the fun times we'd had in Greensboro. Ione and Doug Woodlief also attended. I was so pleased that Wanda Routh Adams, who'd been a bridesmaid in my wedding, traveled from Raleigh with her husband Larue, and Jerry Sumner, who'd been my husband's best man, came with his wife Peggy from Winston-Salem. How intertwined our lives had been, I thought, as we shared memories of those golden days of youth.

There was another reunion that year. In September, I revisited my parents and brother once again. Through the temperature had descended into the 70's, the crepe myrtles were still in bloom as I drove down 220 South. When I arrived in Asheboro, I wondered, what I would discover. Memories of family, wispy as silk threads, spooled through my mind.

I recalled when my parents, my brother, and I lived under the same roof, particularly those years in the gray house with a rock chimney, the house still standing on High Point Street in Randleman. Once a rural mill town and farming community, a

Wal-Mart has now opened there, and soon the town's controversial new dam will be in full operation. How could I avoid smiling as I recalled the childhood pleasures and traumas I'd shared with my parents and brother in that place.

One afternoon, when Mick and I were still in elementary school, we horsed around upstairs in the gray house, attempting to scare one another. My father came up twice, calling us to supper. But Mick and I stayed on, relating the tales we'd heard about Naomi Wise, a town legend. My brother claimed he'd seen her ghost.

I smirked. "Liar, liar, pants on fire," I accused.

Then he elaborated. "It was a young woman," he said, "her face pale, her eyes, glittery green."

Though chill bumps popped up on my arms, I didn't really believe him. But then a white figure bounded into the room. The ghost of Naomi Wise couldn't be that tall, was my first thought.

"Boo," the figure shouted. Every logical bone in my body melted. My brother and I squealed.

Another "Boo" issued from the figure, then a laugh, the raucous unmistakable laughter of Daddy as he jerked the sheet from around him, throwing it aside.

As my Toyota ate a few more miles of highway, I recalled the igloo and fort built by my father from snow blocks formed by a cement block machine. I must have been at least ten years old. Snow had been falling for three days. The yard was a solid sheet of white. Every kid in the neighborhood flocked to our house that afternoon. We used the fort to protect us from snowballs and inside the snow-block igloo, topped by a piece of tin, we pretended to be Eskimos. And I remembered when Daddy played soft ball with us, throwing a knuckle ball that suddenly dived just before reaching the batter. When we complained that we couldn't possibly hit the balls he threw, he let us know that he wasn't there to let us win. "I expect you two to do that on your own."

During the summer, my father's bountiful garden provided most of the vegetables we ate. He took great pleasure in giving away tomatoes to neighbors and friends. How he loved when old Mr. Freeman declared, "Elmer, I swear to mercy, that's the best 'mater I ever et." He also provided food for the table by hunting, accompanied by two clever bird dogs, and by fishing at Pole Cat Creek. Because some questioned his fish stories, he took to cutting off fish heads and storing them in the freezer. If anyone dared doubt the number or length of fish he caught, he'd lead them to the freezer, open it with a flourish, and reveal his fish-head evidence.

My father cherished my mother. We could tell by the way he looked at her, his eyes soulful even if he happened to be lodging a complaint. Often, when she'd be in the kitchen cooking, he'd sneak up behind her and pat her fanny.

Everyone loved mother. Who could help it? Her wide winning smile warms every picture I've ever seen of her. She loved laughing at the antics of babies and puppy dogs. She tee-heed at Elvis Pressley's gyrations on TV, and she roared at stories told by neighbors and friends, always giving them a grander accolade than deserved. And as for her own stories, though she swore they were true, it became obvious to everyone else that her renditions ended up more fiction than fact.

My mother gained enormous satisfaction from simply observing. She often sat on the sofa in our living room, commenting on a particular expression on someone's face, or a nervous gesture. She could recall every word spoken, frequently making more of what had been said than the speaker intended. Instantly her mind would jump to some unfounded conclusion, startling all of us. Once she declared matter-of-factly that a woman who lived in our neighborhood would be leaving her husband within a month.

"Really?" my brother asked. "Did she tell you?"

"There's something different about her eyes," Mother answered with authority. "They're hard. She doesn't look directly at me any more. And that musky cologne she wears now, and she's taken to smoking Camel cigarettes, you know, and wearing high heels, even during the day."

Before my mother finished talking, she'd have invented a story, beginning, middle, and end, including the name of the boyfriend and where the infidels would settle once they ran away. Did my mother's speculations prove true? Rarely, but we loved listening to them anyway.

It would be ungallant of me to write of my mother without mentioning her cooking. She seldom attempted anything fancy, but her butter beans, potatoes, fried chicken, and country style steak could have won ribbons at the state fair, if she'd entered them. Her specialty, though, was cocoanut cream pie. "Pure heaven," my father called it.

My brother Mick remained Mom's biggest fan.

Looking back, I realize why. He was her adorable baby boy, born three years after me. A cuddly soft baby, with auburn curls and brown eyes, he issued agreeable coos. Eventually he became harder. He needed an outer wall to protect him from the world, but always, though he attempted to hide it, there remained an inner vulnerability.

Definitely an over achiever, he had his own way of approaching everything. Once he made up his mind about a person or situation, it became impossible to dissuade him. Always, he loved his family with his whole heart, I believe. Though he would have done anything for us, he didn't do well with looking after himself.

Elected President of his Senior Class at Randleman High School, he also served as Editor of the year book. After graduating, he attended the University of North Carolina at Chapel Hill where he completed undergraduate studies for a B.A. in International Studies. Later he served in the Air Force. Though he stayed in the states during the Viet Nam conflict, apparently out of harm's way, he became ill. After completing his military obligation, he worked as a court reporter in Atlanta, Georgia for a couple of years and then returned to Chapel Hill to attend Law School.

While there, he learned that his illness, spondylitis, a severe arthritis affecting the spine, could not be healed. Little could be done to relieve the pain. Still he worked until his forties, when sickness forced him to retire. By then he took heavy doses of prescribed steroids.

Finally Mick returned home, living in a garage apartment behind our parents' house. During those years he looked after Mom and Dad as they continued on through their seventies. Suddenly their health became fragile. And though Mick rarely complained, his lack of mobility increased and the pain medications he took multiplied.

As I continued down the road that September day in 2006, I

knew it was time for me to be with them again. I'd been away nearly a year. After exiting the 220 bypass in Asheboro, I turned left on Fayetteville Street. Once I reached my destination I slowed, making one final turn. Then driving around a circle, I stopped. This was their place where so many I'd known in Randleman now rested. Carrying a small stool with me, I made my way to the small plot where now my family members are together. "I'm sorry I didn't get here sooner," I apologized. Then putting the stool there beside them, I sat quietly, my head filled with memories.

After I told them what I'd been doing during that year, I left going back to the car. Opening the trunk, I removed a sprightly springtime bouquet of silk daffodils and lilacs. How I wished real flowers were allowed in this place. Going back up the hill, I put the fake flowers in the brass container provided. Closing my eyes, I prayed silently. Then kneeling, I cleaned each of their markers with a soft cloth.

"I love you guys and I miss you," I said. Before leaving the cemetery, I blew them a kiss.

.

Anniversary Waltz

2007 began and ended with dancing.

I love my husband dearly, but he rarely shares my enthusiasm for tripping the light fantastic. I'm certainly not a great dancer, perhaps not even a good one. I have the zeal, yet lack the pizzazz to wow a crowd. Still I adore gliding across a floor, almost as much as I love writing. My own life has, in essence, been a dance, for I've thrown my heart into what I do and I've performed the best I can by relying on some capacity beyond thought and reason.

After years of bugging my husband to take dance lessons, which he sometimes did, but reluctantly, later losing interest, I finally gave up. Beyond the lack of interest, he'd developed bursitis in the hip, which made dancing painful.

But out there existed a solution, I felt certain. Easy as wishing on a speckled toad, I found the answer in January 2007 at Smith Recreation Center, where I participated in senior aerobics. After my exercise session, a flyer tacked to the bulletin board caught my eye: Line Dancing on Tuesday Evenings. Well, of course. Why hadn't I thought of it before? To line dance, a partner isn't required. According to the flyer there would be a free line dance session for any who thought they might be interested.

No one had to twist my arm, or leg.

Mike Summers, an affable mustached man, was the instructor. He also taught square dance and round dance for the city recreation department. He explained and demonstrated each line dance before the class gave it a try. Slow and easy was his approach. Though line dancing is a great aerobic workout, the main purpose, he said, was to have fun. And I did. There's always a new dance to learn. And if you make a misstep, you don't have to worry about stepping on someone's foot.

I line danced through most of 2007, happy to be back on a dance floor. Though I still line dance occasionally, I'm ready to try something new. Maybe belly dancing.

In August of 2007, my husband and I had a special occasion to celebrate—our fiftieth wedding anniversary. I envisioned a gathering of relatives and good friends. We'd break bread together and toast the future. Most of all I wished for an evening to relive with my husband the good times we'd shared.

Joe and I were smart enough to know that a place for an anniversary party wouldn't be available if we waited too long. As early as January, we considered many elegant choices. Wouldn't the new Proximity Hotel be grand? Recently built and known as Greensboro's first "green" hotel, there were few places in Greensboro that could compete with its quiet elegance. When our good friends Johnsie and Bob Hahn threw a celebration for Bob's 70th birthday there, we were quite impressed. Then again, the O'Henry Hotel might work best. The previous year, we'd attended a 50th Anniversary celebration given for our friends

Nancy and Bill Poe. The service had been great and the food delicious.

We also considered at least a dozen other fine celebration sites in Greensboro. Despite the many attractive possibilities, we finally decided on the place that would be just right for us. Bur-Mil Club has rooms to rent for business or social events. Though the building has been around for over fifty years, rooms could be transformed with ribbon, flowers and balloons into something quite grand. So we rented the large banquet room and the one adjoining it for August 17, 2007.

Bur-Mil had for years been a special place for both of us. Practically every week we hiked at least one of the trails there, loving the shade from trees and the tranquil lake view. The park was also the site of many social events we'd attended, including the annual Pig Picking hosted by the Piedmont Hiking and Outing Club. A few times, we'd taken our granddaughter Amber to swim in the pool. Inside the clubhouse we'd attended events as well. As Vice President of the Guilford College Chapter of AARP, I'd recently gone to a State Orientation Meeting held in one of the meeting rooms. Whatever the event, I was always impressed with the cordial treatment and attention to details provided by the staff.

On March 7, planning our anniversary party took the backseat to a more important family event. Our second granddaughter Emily Renee Redding was born.

Our son called from Myrtle Beach shortly after midnight on March 6 to let us know he was taking his wife Tina to the hospital. I had a March 8 deadline for a book review I was writing for the *News & Record*. Resolutely sitting at my desk, I finished the review and sent it to my editor, Elma Sebo, before packing my suitcase.

This second granddaughter wasted no time. Only minutes after Mike and Tina arrived at the hospital, Emily entered our world.

When we sent Jack Hill, a friend who lives in Texas, Emily's infant picture, he emailed back, "That one will be a heart breaker." And she surely will. From the beginning her head was perfectly shaped and covered with dark lustrous hair. She is our smiley girl. Even when her mouth doesn't turn up in a grin, her eyes look out at us with wonder and delight. I know of no experience more calming than holding loveable Emily in my arms.

When she was only a few months old, we had the opportunity to become well acquainted, for we traveled to Myrtle Beach each Tuesday through Friday, for four weeks, to stay with her while her Mom and Dad worked. She spent most of her time sleeping and eating, but, when awake, she loved to be bundled up in the stroller and go for neighborhood rides. She delighted, too, in having her older sister Amber around and Shanna, the cocker spaniel who's the fifth member of my son's family, would allow her any privilege, even letting Emily bite her nose, without snarling back.

We had a busy summer, so plans for the anniversary party, except sending out invitations, were held up until July. After visiting several stores specializing in parties, I finally settled on Partymakers, located on North Main Street. I first met Brenda, the owner of the shop, several years before when I wrote an article about her for *BizLife* magazine.

With Brenda's expert help, I quickly decided on the simple decorations I'd need. I wanted large bouquets of gold balloons to float over the tables. I also wanted those funny stand-ups that I'd rented for parties before. We rented ones of Marilyn Monroe, John Wayne, and, of course, Elvis. Who could have a party without celebrities?

The next question, what would we do for entertainment? Our son Joey plays in a band called "Hot Tin Roof." He agreed to bring mikes and amps and a stereo system so we could hear those golden oldies that had been popular during the year my husband and I married. He also threw in some tunes from the 1960s and 70s. Our youngest son Michael agreed to be MC and make sure everyone had a good time. He also took most of the photographs that evening. And my best hiking buddy, Kittie Schlecht, along with her husband Lowell, warmly greeted and directed guests.

Finally the food. There are many fine catering services in Greensboro, but we settled on Bur-Mil's fine caterer. Bur-Mil also provided the bartender. I shopped for appetizers at the new Fresh Market on Battleground, purchasing scrumptious platters of cheeses and fruits, a platter of veggies, and pita chips served with spinach dip. A home-grown addition to the menu were tomatoes raised by my husband. Plates of them, sliced and lightly salted, were placed at each table.

Finally we were ready to par-tee. Although a few friends couldn't make it, over sixty close friends and family members joined us that evening. We were extremely pleased that four of Joe's sisters—Maxine and her husband J.D. Brookshire, Vera and her husband Bud Cox, Nella and her husband Cletus Lilly, and Rose Parsons were there. Other relatives included Joe's younger brother Thom Redding and his son Chris. They sat at the table with our favorite sister-in-law, Louise Redding, and my cheerful cousins, Linda Richardson, Jean Ritch, Tommy Butler, Sue Butler, and Nancy Butler.

When our son asked if anyone would stand up and say

something about us, I was overwhelmed by the response. Some remembered long ago incidents that I had forgotten; some of the comments were so touching they brought tears to my eyes. And some were remembrances of funny or embarrassing moments. My lovely cousin, Linda Richardson, entertained everyone with her storytelling talent. Our friend Joanna Price said she recalled that once I danced on a table. Much as I love dancing, I don't recall ever going *that* far.

That evening I read an essay I'd written for my husband. My granddaughter Amber drew a picture of a rainbow to go with it, which I framed to give him. And, wonder of wonder, Joe actually danced with me.

What an unforgettable evening.

Two days later we went to Asheville, continuing our trip back through time. While there, we dropped by the Battery Park Hotel, where we'd spent our honeymoon. We were surprised to discover that the grand old hotel is now a retirement home. One of the residents, delighted to hear why we were there, gave us a tour. Though impressed, we still prefer living in our own home, and though those cool mountain breezes would be refreshing in August, Asheville, at least to us, still doesn't compare to Greensboro.

THANKS FOR THE RAINBOWS

Read to my husband, Joseph Redding, on our 50th Wedding Anniversary, 8/17/08

When Amber, our granddaughter, visited us in August, my husband and I had a great time entertaining her. Each evening she wanted to feed the ducks at the Bog Garden, and afterwards we'd go for ice cream at Maxie B's.

Grandpop never said, "No" to Amber. The two of them had a blast. She amused him with songs and stories. He showed her how to fly his remote-control airplane. Their laughter filled our house as they played computer games. Amber and Grandpop share an exceptional relationship. I believe they always will.

Like Amber, I, too, adore Grandpop. Probably for the same reasons.

On Friday, the day before she left, going back home to her parents in Myrtle Beach, I came down with a stomach virus. The next day, Joe drove Amber home while I stayed behind, feeling absolutely miserable.

By Monday morning, I'd lost five pounds. Though considerably better, I lacked my usual zip-a-dee-do-da. Because

Joe had to leave for a business trip, he was concerned about me. I assured him I'd be fine. Still, sorry for myself, I felt sad as he drove away on Monday morning. Before I had time to crawl back into bed, the phone rang. My husband spoke, his voice filled with enthusiasm. "Hello, Dear," he said. "Go outside. There's the prettiest rainbow I've ever seen."

After promising I would, I reluctantly relinquished my pillow and stumbled out the front door in my purple pajamas. Sure enough, a glorious rainbow stretched from the rooftop of our neighbor's house, arching across the road, finally ending a few houses away. The intensity of the brilliant colors hurt my eyes. Amazed that a mere rainbow had the power to buoy my lagging spirit, I smiled and almost wept.

And therein lays the secret of a happy marriage, at least from my perspective.

Enduring relationships weather icy days and times of drought. Refreshing as spring, hard times are balanced by periods of renewal and growth. And similar to summer, the best marriages are blessed by days of warmth and passion.

As a child, I believed angels were weeping when it rained. But rain, whether real or metaphorical, provides more than adequate compensations. Among the rewards, I particularly cherish, are the rare sighting of rainbows. Rainbows offer hope and possibility. Though we might not see the sun, we know it's there.

Tonight, standing here, I feel that I'm one lucky woman. Not only does my husband believe in rainbows, he searches diligently for them. Then he calls, sharing the good news: "Dear, go outside. See how beautiful."

Dance Instructions

Dancing is more than rhythmic leaps, glides, and dips. True, dance requires movement, but movement without emotion isn't dance. A dancer's heart must beat with joy; her gestures must tell a story; and her entire body must vibrate with enthusiasm as she prances and shimmies.

Determined to live as if every day is a new dance, I see dance everywhere: clouds *glide* across the sky, raindrops *caper* onto rooftops, and excited squirrels *leap* here, there, everywhere to avoid oncoming vehicles capable of ending their dance.

For those, like me, wishing to dance through the hours, days and years, instruction is recommended. Through the decades, I've depended on many for guidance. Here I've included a few current instructors. All live or have lived in Greensboro.

Choreography is the heart of dance. There must be a beginning plan for the performance, though the plan often changes, improving over time. My friend Cathie Holcombe understands the necessity of choreography for dance, and life.

A few years ago, the broad view of what Cathie's next dance

would be occurred in Honduras. While she and her husband Rob helped other Habitat for Humanity volunteers construct houses, she noticed Honduran children nearby. The sweetness of their laughter amazed her, for they had so little, yet they found joy in something as simple as rolling a tire down the road. Her heart warmed to them. She wondered what she might do to help. Soon she planned the first steps of the choreography. Cathie decided to become a volunteer, teaching in a Honduran primary school for a year. To do so, she had to learn Spanish. During the time she taught in Honduras, she added new steps to her routine. The school needed books. She wrote to friends, letting them know. Eventually, she provided a library for the school, enough books so that every child could take one home to read. Her dance then became even more difficult and beautiful. She met a young man in Honduras who possessed the ability to make a great difference in his country, but because he was from a large family, he lacked the financial resources to bring his dream to fruition.

Cathie, after sorting through a mountain of red tape, finally managed to bring Marvin Redondo to Greensboro where he studied English at the Interlink Language Center of the University of North Carolina. On December 21, 2007, he received his certificate of completion and has now returned to Santa Cruz where, he says, he plans to be mayor some day.

Today, Cathie's choreographed dance with Honduras continues, influencing more and more people to reach out helping others. When I interviewed her for two articles I published in my *News & Record* column, I understood, after hearing her story, how crucial planning is to reaching any goal.

Ironically, though my husband Joe doesn't care to dance, he's become my best teacher. **Persistence** makes all things possible might well be his motto. Though now seventy, he still pursues tasks with gusto. I've seen him work for hours to solve a computer problem without giving up. When he begins a project around the house, he never stops until it's finished.

When my brother Mick lay dying at Wesley Long Hospital, I felt that it was important for someone to be there with him. Though my husband worked full-time, he would come each evening to relieve me during the night, so I could rest. Exhausted, I felt that I couldn't go on at one point, but he assured me that by working together, someone would be by my brother's bed until the day he died. Once again I was deeply impressed with my husband's ability to go the distance.

Music is essential to the dance I advocate. Not necessarily external music blaring from a stereo or the loud music of a Rock 'n Roll band. Instead, it's internal music that keeps one moving in the right direction. My friend Lundee Amos has caught the beat that keeps her smiling. The music within also keeps Lundee busier than anyone I know. She scampers off with the Friendship Force to Peru, then she's flying away to visit her sister in California. We briefly talk while hiking, and then she's off again, this time headed to Hickory to look after her grandsons.

The music that carries Lundee is contagious. Because she loves musicians she schedules jam sessions in her spacious home. Nearly a hundred people, sometimes even more, show up to listen and to share food. Many of her guests come just to be around Lundee. A healing touch practitioner, she encourages with kindness and hugs. There's no finer music.

In dance and life, it's often the **details** that transform an ordinary performance into an extraordinary one. A dancer doesn't just hold her head up; she must hold her head at a precise angle as her toes point and flex. And if the dancer doesn't jump into her partner's arms at the right moment, she sinks to the floor. The costume must be just so, and the make-up and hair must be appropriate to the performance. A successful dance depends on multiple details, and it takes a perfectionist to get it right.

My friend Kathryn Lovatt, who now lives in South Carolina, always knows just what to do, whether it's cooking an extraordinary meal, renovating an historic home, or planning a wedding. Though I've always admired the perfection of Kathryn's touch, reflected in all she does, it's most evident in the short stories she writes. Her choice of just-right physical descriptions, gestures, and dialogue bring her southern characters alive. A superb editor, she intuitively knows what needs to be kept and what needs to be discarded in the stories of others as well as her own.

To be a dancer requires stamina, so being **physically fit** is essential. I've relied heavily on the Greensboro Recreation Department for help. A member of AHOY, I join other senior citizens at Lindley, Smith or Lewis Recreation Center for aerobics three times a week. This free exercise program, usually led by always helpful Cindy Hipp, not only helps tone sagging muscles but also enhances the spirit.

I also belong to the Senior Walkers. On Wednesday morning, the group hikes either locally in one of Greensboro's tranquil parks or greenways or goes out of town by van or bus to explore other North Carolina hiking sites. Of all exercise, hiking remains my first love, so I also hike with the Crafty Cruisers, an inspiring group of men and women, usually led by the indomitable Bill

Craft. And both my husband and I have been members of the Piedmont Hiking and Outing Club for more than fifteen years. Though I no longer attempt their long hikes, those over ten miles, I still enjoy shorter treks and socials with these fine folks.

At least a couple of times a week my husband and I get out in the woods, which we consider a sacred venture. Sometimes our long-time hiking buddies Kittie Schlecht, Bob Hahn, Hermann Trojanowski, and Ruth Heybrock accompany us. It's a great way to keep fit while staying in touch with friends who mean a great deal.

Another resource I depend on for exercise is Adventures in Learning sponsored by Greensboro Shepherd's Center. Through this senior citizen program, I've taken yoga, folk dancing, line dancing and sit-down exercises. Offering courses for the mind as well as the body, Shepherd's Center provides a variety of instruction in such diverse areas as science, woodcarving, and financial planning.

Another quality that enhances dancing is for the dancers to **share a bond** with their partners. This can't be faked, for those watching will detect the slightest false note. Additionally the dancer, to be successful, must form a bond with the audience.

When thinking of connections, I'm reminded of my neighbor, Iris Jones. After my husband and I moved to Efland Drive, next door to her and her husband Bob, we would always see the two of them together. Because we knew how close they were, we worried about Iris when Bob died a few years ago.

Though Iris missed Bob, she has, over the years, formed strong lasting bonds with many others, particularly her children, her grandchildren, and her sister. She also nurtures a wide circle of friends, including neighbors and the women who attend her church. Whenever one of Iris' grandchildren has an accident, a ball game, or a graduation, she hops into her car, hurrying to be there. This past year, Iris joined together with women in her church, making hundreds of pillows. She then traveled with her friends to John Hopkins Hospital. There, they personally formed new bonds of caring by distributing some of their hand-made pillows to hospitalized veterans.

One final tidbit of advice. **Take care of the basics**. For dancing that means pampering your feet. Invest in comfortable shoes and pedicures. Make a political statement with your toenails. Paint them red or blue. Even better, paint them green. In one article I wrote for the *News & Record* a few years ago, I claimed that my feet were my best body part. Now, at age sixty-nine, that's still true. Feet are absolutely essential. How would we glide across the floor without them?

Happy Feet

2008, what a grand year for Greensboro! Thanks to the innovative planning of the Bicentennial Commission Co-chairs, Claudette Burroughs, Al Lineberry, Jr. and Elizabeth (Boo) Stauffer, those of us residing here now have an even greater appreciation for this *green* place we call home.

The first party began the evening of March 28, at First Horizon Park, following a torch relay that extended throughout the city. Greensboro's recently elected Mayor, Yvonne Johnson, welcomed one and all. Music filled the air and men dressed as Revolutionary soldiers stood guard as our mayor read the proclamation. When the last relay runner lit the caldron, the crowd roared and gleeful children spilled out onto the field, delighting one and all. Soon horns blared, drums rolled, and skydivers drifted down from the sky.

A celebration without dancing? No way. The three sprightly Bicentennial mascots, one costumed in a 2 and the others in zero's, forming 200, lifted their happy feet, performing a Bicentennial Hop.

In April, the festivities continued with a Heritage Festival, recognizing the history and various cultures represented in our fair city. In downtown Greensboro, the town crier shouted the news as talented artists displayed crafts and music groups from blue grass to gospel to Rock 'n Roll performed. Dancers representing many ethnic groups, including African, Scottish, and Chinese, had the crowd clapping and stomping their feet.

Neighborhoods celebrated with block parties. Guided tours through older sections of town and cemeteries renewed citizens' interest in history. Lectures held at the public library on topics as diverse as Greensboro's noted writers and the railroad drew huge crowds. Plays held at the Historical Museum and Poetry Readings at the Carolina Theatre entertained and awed.

During May, at the Greensboro Coliseum Pavilion, the World of Tomorrow Science and Technology Expo provided a glimpse of Greensboro's future. Hybrid cars, the latest in medical technology, and a futuristic glimpse of how to order perfect shoes were only a few of the innovative exhibits. Entertaining the child in all of us, streams of colored laser light bounced across walls and onto the ceiling. Elsewhere, providing a salute to the past, archaeological digs conducted at Blandwood and the Bicentennial Garden uncovered pieces of Greensboro's past.

What's a celebration without a parade? A grand procession, depicting Greensboro's past, present, and future took place on July 4th. Bands, motorcycles, fire trucks, vintage cars, clowns and the town crier provided a cacophony of sounds as floats transported Greensboro's city officials, beauty queens, athletes, and church choirs. A bevy of dancers, including ballerinas and a troupe called Ladybugs, twirled and swayed down the street. After the sun set, patriotic music filled every corner of downtown.

As fireworks exploded, grateful citizens rose to their feet, offering a unified roar of appreciation.

In addition to star-studded entertainment, the Bicentennial events also brought a deeper sense of continuity to those living here. Gatherings in churches to share various faiths strengthened collective spirituality. Learning more about Greensboro's past increased pride. The solidarity of the various ethnic, economic, and religious groups represented in managing, staffing and volunteering the celebration transformed into reality the long-held belief that all citizens could join together, working peacefully toward a common goal.

Last year, my gift to the city was continuing to interview and write about people living in Greensboro. For the past two years, Cindy Loman, one of the talented editors of the *News & Record*, has published my profiles of superior senior citizens. Now, by writing this book, I have continued my mission: paying homage to my home town by celebrating her greatest asset, the people who live, work, play and love here.

This year I enjoyed helping to blow out the 200 candles topping Greensboro's birthday cake. Next August, I intend to blow out the seventy flaming tapers topping my own. On that day I'll remember again my childhood dream of dancing down the street of Greensboro wearing new red shoes. After putting on my green dancing slippers, I'll take my husband's hand. "Let's go downtown," I'll tell him. "It's time to dance."

Here's hoping you'll join our celebration.

Printed in the United States
206269BV00001B/334-486/P